Praise for

BeyondtheSling

"*Beyond the Sling* is a delightful look into the parenting journey Mayim is making with her husband. Her family-first stories are an inspiring reminder of how we navigated these waters ourselves. We have learned that when parents choose to parent with attachment in mind, they make a lot of other good, holistic decisions regarding the health and well-being of the family. She invites her readers to understand attachment parenting, see how it is working for her family, and choose what can work for their own."

—William Sears, MD, and Martha Sears, RN, coauthors of
The Baby Book and *The Attachment Parenting Book*

"As an outspoken advocate for childbirth choices, I have worked tirelessly to educate parents about their birthing options. With *Beyond the Sling*, Mayim Bialik has developed a fantastic guide to birth and to parenting that is packed with invaluable wisdom. At once conversational, informative, and progressive, this book should be compulsory reading for anyone who has even considered becoming a parent."

—Ricki Lake, executive producer of *The Business of
Being Born* and author of *Your Best Birth*

"*Beyond the Sling* goes beyond the scope of the standard books to enhance the parenting experience. Mayim's warmth, dedication, and professionalism are felt throughout this wonderful book."

—Lauren Feder, MD, author of *Natural Baby and Childcare*
and *The Parents' Concise Guide to Childhood Vaccinations*

"Drawing on her education as a neuroscientist, her instinct as a mother, and a community of support, Mayim has passionately embraced attachment parenting principles for raising her children. In *Beyond the Sling* she shows how the secure attachment relationship that she has developed with her children has given her the confidence to define her own natural parenting style."

—Barbara Nicholson and Lysa Parker, cofounders of
Attachment Parenting International and
coauthors of *Attached at the Heart*

BeyondtheSling

A Real-Life Guide to Raising Confident,

Loving Children the Attachment Parenting Way

Mayim Bialik, PhD, CLEC

A Touchstone Book

Published by Simon & Schuster

New York   London   Toronto   Sydney   New Delhi

Touchstone
A Division of Simon & Schuster, Inc.
1230 Avenue of the Americas
New York, NY 10020

First Touchstone trade paperback edition September 2012

TOUCHSTONE and colophon are registered trademarks of Simon & Schuster, Inc.

For information about special discounts for bulk purchases, please contact Simon & Schuster Special Sales at 1-866-506-1949 or business@simonandschuster.com.

The Simon & Schuster Speakers Bureau can bring authors to your live event. For more information or to book an event contact the Simon & Schuster Speakers Bureau at 1-866-248-3049 or visit our website at www.simonspeakers.com.

Photograph on page 16 designed by Maia Rosenfeld.
Other photographs courtesy of the author.

Designed by Ruth Lee-Mui

Manufactured in the United States of America

5   7   9   10   8   6   4

Library of Congress Cataloging-in-Publication Data

Bialik, Mayim.
Beyond the sling : a real-life guide to raising confident, loving children the attachment parenting way / Mayim Bialik.
        p.   cm.
"A Touchstone Book."
Includes bibliographical references and index.
1. Child rearing. 2. Parenting. I. Title.
HQ769.B5723 2012
649'.122—dc23

2011026778

ISBN 978-1-4516-1800-6
ISBN 978-1-4516-6218-4 (pbk)
ISBN 978-1-4516-1801-3 (ebook)

למאיר ראש ואפרים הירש
שהפכו אותי למאמע
"נצור לשונך מרע ושפתיך מדבר מרמה
סור מרע ועשה טוב בקש שלום ורודפהו"

For Miles Roosevelt (Meir Rosh) and
Frederick Heschel (Ephraim Hirsch)
who made me a Mama

"Guard your tongue from evil and your lips from speaking deceit;
Turn from evil and do good, seek Peace and pursue It."
Psalm 34

Contents

Part III: What Baby Doesn't Need   119

Part IV: What Mommy Needs   203

Introduction

We can do better.

I've seen far too many articles and books about so-called good enough parenting. Why settle for "good enough"? This book will show you how to excel at parenting—and how to enjoy yourself and your baby along the way—through a parenting style called "attachment parenting."

As a pediatrician, I occasionally have very difficult two-month-old checkups with new parents who seem to confront and dislike every step of the first weeks of life: "How could she need to eat *again*?" or "How could he need *another* diaper?"

I try to gently guide them into realizing that at 3:00 a.m. there are options: you can clench your teeth, roll your eyes, and sigh during those wake-ups (and probably lose another half hour's sleep from worry and agitation). Or you can wake up with a big grin to greet your child and say out loud, "Hello, my sweet hungry baby. Again!"

A true story: some years ago I had two consecutive two-week exams scheduled one morning. I picked up the first chart and read my nurse's notes about a very unhappy and stressed mom and dad.

Their beautiful little girl had gained 3 to 4 ounces over her birth weight (which is just fine!). But during our appointment they tearfully told me how they couldn't believe that their baby needed to eat every two hours all night long, and how she slept only brief intervals during the day, and everything was just so hard, and they hadn't expected this, and they weren't sure Mom had enough milk and . . . It was a tough visit. I think we finally reached a little smiling time at the end as we tried to focus on wonderful weight gain, good pee and poop, and normal milestones.

In the next room, the second two-week-old had also gained a few ounces over birth weight, but the nurse's notes read, "Sleeps through the night." That's physiologically abnormal and a little worrisome. I was sure something was wrong.

They told me no, they were giving her only breast milk, frequent feeds, lots of pee and poop, and yes, she slept through the night. I argued for a few minutes. Finally this tired mom and dad insisted yes, she sleeps straight through the night. They said, "She gets up to feed every couple hours or so, but she sleeps through the night!"

I wished I had a little camera running to shoot this. The second family's perception of their nighttime adventures feeding their weight-gaining, developmentally sound, and happy daughter was that—in spite of their being awake every two hours or so for nursing—the baby was sleeping through the night! They were learning to adjust to their baby's rhythms with love and a relaxed (albeit sleep-deprived) equanimity about their daughter's needs. I think the first mother and father had either read the wrong books, had some tough-love advice whispered (shouted?) in their ears, or just weren't quite prepared for the relentless emotional responsibility of caring for a newborn.

Parenting is a lot of work. My advice: don't shy away from it. Instead, attach yourselves. Wrap your lives around your newborns' lives and rhythms and realize that, rather than returning to "normalcy," this *is* the new normal.

Try to just plain love the increasing responsiveness and the extra eye contact and the teeny attempts your baby makes to smile at you in those first few weeks. Get absolutely delighted when those tiny (gassy?) smiles turn into big purposeful grins at you in the fifth or sixth or seventh week. Love the poop. Love the poop?! Yes, even the poop!

A parent's instincts will guide you and even comfort and reassure you better than the advice of any doctor, grandparent, or friend. If your baby looks good, nurses a lot, pees, poops, makes eye contact, smiles some weeks later, moves and squirms and cuddles to sleep in Mom's arms and Dad's arms? That's a great baby.

Attach yourself to this baby and embrace his or her nascent relationship with you as the family grows. Some bestselling books actually ask you to make your relationship with your baby *smaller* month by month: "Try to get your infant to eat a little less, sleep a little longer, be picked up a little less." They say, "Don't feed her because she's hungry, feed her because it's exactly two o'clock. Don't pick him up when he's crying; he has to learn that you're going to teach him to soothe himself back to sleep." And what does that teach your baby . . . that his mom and dad, the two people in the whole world you can count on day and night, 24/7, to be there and love you, really *aren't* there when you're scared at 3 a.m. or hungry a little earlier than the books say you should be?

How have we let "crying it out" and schedule feeding become the cultural norm? How have we convinced parents that loving their children consistently and persistently when they need us will spoil them? Now, I do believe that you can spoil a three- or four-year-old child if he whines and yells and gets a cookie. But you *can't* spoil a baby! When babies cry, they're really just talking to us, expressing the most basic human and physiological needs for nourishment, warmth, cuddles, trust.

Break this cycle. Buy *this* book and learn and feel how wonderful it is to respond and hug and cuddle and nurse and listen to your baby's new "words" and facial expressions and so much more.

I've seen "detached" families, too. They don't function well. The parents don't know their kids that well, and when it comes time to set important limits and boundaries, the foundation just isn't there.

Build the biggest possible relationship for when it *does* come time to set some boundaries and limits for your older baby or toddler. You might pick nine or twelve or fifteen months of age to look your baby in the eye and express the sentiments that she's *not* actually the empress of a large nation but instead a very, very beloved member of a family . . . and that she might have to wait four or five minutes while oatmeal is being cooked or apples are pureed. And try as you might, she may cry. But I view this as demotion from a ten-foot pedestal to a nine-foot pedestal. And at these ages, you have a big, powerful little baby or toddler who can withstand that demotion based on the astounding amount of love, closeness, and attachment of the first year of life.

This book has everything: it has the science, the feeling, the emotion, the logic, and the best advice you'll ever receive about . . . *harder* parenting?? No!! Intuitive, loving parenting leading the sweet, smart, happy baby, toddler, child, teen you always knew you'd raise.

This is a very personal book. Mayim has written about her own family, Miles and Fred, the most active, self-confident boys you'd ever want to meet. In the midst of a pleasant conversation, you realize that's it just four or five people sitting around talking, all of us expressing our thoughts and feelings and more. A closer look reveals that two of the people are only three or four feet tall and a little less articulate than the rest, but they're people, raised to reflect the respect and love they've felt and been immersed in for years. They understand communication and they understand limits and they are just plain fun to hang out around with. They have been raised by attachment parents, and I think you'll like this style and this book a lot.

JAY GORDON, MD, FAAP

Part I

Trust Your Instincts

1

You Know More Than You Think

Ah, parenthood. Guiding a little soul through its infancy. Caressing tiny chubby fingers by moonlight. Molding a person from start to finish, and seeing only goodness and satisfaction reflected back at you every single time that your child breathes, speaks, and smiles. Creating a miniature version of you, only better, smarter, wiser, and more fashionable! Isn't this what your life as a parent looks like?

Yeah, I didn't think so. Mine doesn't look like that, either.

Don't get me wrong: I love being a parent. My two sons have stolen a piece of my heart and brain; they occupy a sacred part of my entire being and will do so forever. However, I also find parenting incredibly challenging, utterly exhausting, downright frustrating, and often crazy-making.

Part of what is so confusing is all the conflicting advice we parents get, from all angles: our parents, our friends, our doctors, our baby books, various "experts," even perfect strangers on the street. Everyone's got an opinion, and no one is shy about sharing it with us.

But if you are anything like me, you don't have a predetermined set of decisions about child rearing laid out. Furthermore, you get confused when you are given dozens of different answers to one seemingly simple question, especially if each answer sounds reasonable, is backed by research, and is delivered by someone you like and trust. A whole parenting industry has been created, it seems, solely to confuse us.

We are told to hold our babies—but don't hold them too much! Or should we hold them *more?* (There's research supporting both assertions.)

We're advised to sleep close to them—but not too close! (You'll find vocal supporters on both sides of this argument as well.)

We're recommended to hold them and comfort them—but not too much, because they have to also learn to self-soothe! (But how much is too much? And is my kid the same as yours?)

And on and on and on. It's enough to make you wonder how anyone ever reaches first grade without the need for a pediatric psychologist living in their home to help sort through all of this insanity.

Parenting books number in the tens of thousands, each promising you comprehensive help raising the "best" child in the quickest amount of time, and specialty books seeking to solve "once and for all" the most persistent of parenting concerns such as sleep and feeding. I read those books when I was first pregnant, and I have read dozens of them throughout the past seven years. Some of what I read has helped me, but most of what I read has made me feel overwhelmed, incompetent, and sometimes wrong for doing what I wanted to do. I know I'm not alone in feeling this way.

This is not that kind of parenting book.

What I have discovered, and what I seek to share with you, dear reader, is this: *you already know the majority of what you need to know to be an incredible parent.* It was only when I believed this and began to apply it consistently to my growing family that my anxiety, worry, and exhaustion began to lift. It was then that I truly began to enjoy being a parent and to see myself as a successful parent; not a perfect parent, and not always the most patient parent, but a sensitive, loving, and confident parent who truly loves this life I have chosen. That's really what this book is about: empowering you to make the best choices for your kids.

So what exactly have I chosen for my kids? I have figured out what works for our family, and the basic idea is this: hundreds of thousands of years of evolution have prepared all of us, should we so choose, to be a parent. A good parent! Not a perfect parent but the best parents we can be. The knowledge we need is already programmed into our DNA.

But trends in the past two hundred years or so of Western culture have convinced us that we need *a lot* of help: help giving birth; help choosing what to feed the baby; help "teaching" our baby to sleep, to eat, and to learn; help making the baby independent as soon as humanly possible; help just *being* a parent. I propose that we, for the most part, need very little of this kind of help in these matters. By understanding basic theories of attachment and infant development, by surrounding ourselves with a community (and a culture) that seeks to support healthy and natural choices that make intuitive sense, and by trusting that everything a baby needs is communicated honestly, simply, and without malice or manipulation, we can truly be the parents that nature intends us to be.

A baby tells us exactly what he needs in his own language. Our job is to learn to speak that language. That's what this book is all about.

I Didn't Start Out This Way

So did all of this come naturally to me? Am I some sort of natural "earth mother" who was effortlessly able to tap in to my children's innermost needs? Was I raised in an immersive attachment parenting environment, a style of parenting that I simply mimicked when I was blessed with children?

In a word, no.

Before I had kids, I had decided that parenting was not going to be that hard. People who talked about their kids all the time tended to bore me. I questioned their choice of time management as I shook my head sadly at their apparent lack of adult recreational activities. Did they really want to use all of their time reading about parenting? Perhaps they had social problems or maybe even an anxiety disorder, since they clearly had nothing better to do than hang out with their babies while their friends went to Las Vegas or relaxed at the spa. Had they not read "the book" on parenting? Why were they making it all seem like such hard work? In my opinion, they were giving parenting a very bad name.

The knowledge I have now came from backing off on my defensiveness and judgment, opening my mind to hearing new ideas, doing a lot of reading and study, and talking honestly with both friends and experts. Much of my formulation of parenting, though, has come as the result of a lot of hard-won practice and experience raising my two young boys, Miles and Frederick.

My grandparents were immigrants from war-torn Eastern Europe preceding World War II, and they came to America poor, uneducated, and brokenhearted because of the life and family they had to leave behind. My parents were born during World War II and were raised in the Bronx as assimilated American Jews. From what I have pieced together, my grandparents' style of child rearing was strict, assertive, and somewhat authoritarian. Both of my parents attended public college in the 1960s in New York, and they soon became part of the political and social upheaval of that era that made them more enlightened, more open-minded, and more liberal than anyone in their families. They ate health food and lived a bohemian lifestyle in the West Village, making documentaries against the Vietnam War and traveling to Washington, DC, for antiwar protests.

Okay, I'll just say it: my parents were hippies.

My liberated feminist mother, once she got around to convincing herself that having kids would not end her life (or convincing herself that all the fun was over anyway, so why not have kids), delivered me with no pain medication or interventions of any kind. She tried cloth diapering, but I was allergic to her detergent. When she stopped breast-feeding me, she fed me soymilk instead of cow's milk, because she didn't want to feed me "the milk of another animal," as she put it. Pretty ahead of her time, right? And when I requested bottle after bottle at night, my mother sweetly obliged rather than let me "cry it out." Looking back, she wishes she had the support to bring me back into her bed.

My parents' progressiveness did not extend to all aspects of child rearing. Blessed as I am to have these wacky, funny, and irreverent people as my sperm and egg donors, certain aspects of their parenting style looked more like *their* parents' than even they would have liked to admit. It was a pleasant dictatorship of sorts with a lot of perks to the subject (me), but for the most part, my parents usually told me when I was cold, tired, hungry, upset, or happy, even if I didn't necessarily agree.

This parent-centered style of that era continued into my adolescence and young adulthood, as my precocious (and, looking back, rather naive) interest in being an actress took me in two short years from success in an elementary school play to a critically acclaimed role as the young Bette Midler in the 1989 film *Beaches*. Shortly thereafter, I was starring in my own NBC sitcom, *Blossom*.

My parents guided my career and managed every aspect of it, which was appropriate, helpful, and necessary. Their parenting style carried over into their management style: our relationship continued to be hierarchically structured, with me as the one in the relationship with a somewhat "lower" status, since, being a child, I indeed knew less than my parents about both show business and adult interactions. People are often surprised to hear that my parents and I functioned this way *before* I became an actress and that my career did not precipitate their being as authoritative as they appeared; it was actually as if our "pleasant dictatorship" was designed to manufacture precocious sitcom actresses! I look back at those years fondly, and I felt that I was protected by my parents as much in my home as I was on a television set.

At the end of the five-year run of *Blossom*, at nineteen, I decided to leave acting and pursue a degree in neuroscience and Hebrew and Jewish studies. My parents were supportive, but had I not been a legal adult, they might have liked me to continue acting. As an undergraduate at UCLA, I met a tall and quiet young man who looked like Elvis Costello, liked racquetball as much as I did, and seemed to enjoy my cooking, my intellectual interests, and my oddball sense of humor. We dated for five years and both started graduate school in 2000: me in neuroscience specializing in hormones of bonding, attachment, and obsessive-compulsive disorder; and he in political science, specializing in American politics. We married in 2003 and had Miles while still in graduate school. Frederick was born ten months after I submitted my thesis (can you say "celebration baby"?).

Now, I am sure you are saying, "Look at your list of successes: you turned out okay despite the parent-centered philosophy of your upbringing!" (while secretly hoping that you, the reader, turned out okay, too), and I suppose that this is largely true. However, when I talk with my mother, my husband's mother, and many women of this era, they often report that they spent their first years as parents utterly confused, frustrated, and overwhelmed with feelings of inadequacy. They were told that babies eat only every four hours, but we were hungry every two. They were told not to sleep with a baby, but we cried when we were not held close. They were told to get back to life and "get over" their doubts, their questions, and their sense of unease. But something tugged at their minds, and at their hearts, and they could not simply get over it.

It is this kind of tug that I argue ought to be listened to. Parents today are still being told the same kinds of things by authority figures with fancy degrees: when to hold the baby, when not to hold the baby, how to hold the baby, how not to hold the baby, why to hold the baby, why not to hold the baby, and so on. Parents hear this advice from doctors, nurses, and passersby on the street alike (I know I did and still do):

"You'll spoil the baby if you hold him too much."

"Babies won't learn to crawl if you don't frustrate them by letting them fuss and struggle in a crib; they'll never be motivated."

"If you meet all of a baby's needs too promptly, she'll never learn to ask for anything and may have speech delays."

"Your child has to reach these milestones or he will have to see a speech therapist/physical therapist/occupational therapist."

"If you don't start solids now, your baby will never eat."

Really? Something didn't seem right about a parenting style governed by fear and uncertainty. There had to be a better way.

Finding My Own Parenting Style

Attachment parenting (AP) is the loose set of guidelines that started to resonate with me both as I did research about parenting and as I pursued my degree in neuroscience. As a "green" person in regard to how I ate, shopped, and cleaned my apartment, I came to understand that there is also such a thing as "green parenting." A green style of parenting seeks to create a generation of children who love and respect people and the earth because they have been loved and respected by their parents. Look to societies where the environment is neglected and abused, and you will find that children's well-being is also often neglected. Look to countries where environmentalism is a way of life for all people, and you may be surprised to find that these countries also spend tremendous resources to ensure the optimal development of happy and bonded families.

So what is attachment parenting really about? Attachment Parenting International (API) identifies AP as guided by eight principles. The practical application varies greatly but it often looks something like this:

1. **Birth:** Prepare for birth and become educated about natural birth options and their benefits for baby and mother.
2. **Breastfeeding/breast milk:** A human mother's milk is the optimal food for human babies, and bottle feeding should mimic as many aspects of breastfeeding as possible.
3. **Be sensitive:** Respond sensitively to your children.
4. **Bonding through touch:** Use physical contact such as baby wearing, breastfeeding, and massage to convey tenderness, love, and affection.
5. **Bedding:** Parent your children at night as well as in the day, looking to safe co-sleeping as an option.
6. **Be there:** Ensure consistent parenting by a primary caregiver or a trained and sensitive substitute.
7. **Be gentle:** Use positive discipline, forgoing corporal punishment.
8. **Balance:** Balance your needs with those of your child.

It should be noted that no one does all eight perfectly, nor do you have to subscribe to all of them to benefit from these principles. These are simply guidelines that can serve as a jumping-off place for your decision-making. There are families who differ in many aspects of these principles, and there are no "attachment police" who revoke your membership if they catch your child asleep in his own bed. In addition, attachment parenting is not, contrary to popular belief, a parenting style just for people who are wealthy or who are at-home parents, nor is it for people with an abnormal or superhuman amount of patience. It is for people from all walks of life who seek to parent gently and who believe that an independent adult is one who was allowed to form a healthy dependence and attachment to her caregiver in her formative years.

What I discovered as an observer of families who lived by the principles of attachment parenting was that they did not bow to those who tried to coerce, threaten, mock, or cause fear about the most natural and instinctual event on the planet: being a parent. The relationships they had with their children were reciprocally considerate, respectful, loving, and authentic. The adults made choices about their pregnancies, births, and lifestyles out of a sense of faith, courage, and empowerment. They did not yell or use force to be heard by their children, and their children were receptive to being guided in their activities and behaviors without being afraid to assert their needs.

What I discovered about attachment parenting as a neuroscientist was even more surprising and led me to a sort of internal revelation: these principles make sense evolutionarily. They foster brain development, promote healthy and secure attachment, and produce relationships that are scientifically proven to be sound in terms of infant health, psychological achievement, and the ability to truly thrive. By this reasoning, everything I had been taught from evolutionary biology all the way up to advanced neuroanatomy and neuropsychiatry supports the following: these principles do not need to be taught. Rather, they are innate, having been whittled down and programmed into our genetic code over hundreds of thousands of years of trial and error. The first Homo sapiens knew the same things I know about how to be a parent, even if it seems that I only intuitively know that the baby needs to stay alive and that it's my job to make that happen.

My training in neuroscience and years of anecdotal observation led me to the crux of the style of parenting I will describe in this book: there is something in us that already knows what our babies need. As prospective parents, we are bombarded with conflicting evidence, staggering statistics, threats of babies "too clingy" or "not securely attached" or—worse yet—psychologically harmed forever by our best intentions. We meet with obstetricians, midwives, pediatricians, child development psychologists, marital counselors, and preschool administrators. We turn to friends, books, and even well-meaning family members to help us parent the "right way," but what is right for one family is not always right for another. And there is a primal, ancient, and elegant instinct that we can tap in to to be the best parents we can be. This is not an easy task. Our instinct has been buried and smothered in recent years. It has been dismissed, mocked, ridiculed, and slandered. It has been the basis of spousal disputes, family battles, and internal wars. How do we get this instinct back?

How to Use This Book

When I started along the path of attachment parenting, the documented resources available to me were scant. *Mothering* magazine, La Leche League International (LLLI), and our brave and brilliant pediatrician were our only sources for facts, figures, advice, and support. Organizations like the Holistic Moms Network and API gained my membership because these communities were open to sharing attachment parenting wisdom and experience free of judgment. But I did not find books by real moms or dads about what this lifestyle actually looks like.

It occurred to me that others might like to hear how it works for us, and that's really how this book was born. I do not claim to have the formula for raising the perfect child. My kids are flawed and they make plenty of mistakes, as do I. My kids are not always polite, patient, clean, wise, and quiet; nor am I, for that matter. If there were a formula for raising the quietest/happiest/gentlest/easiest/best/ sweetest/most generous and polite child, it would have been figured out thousands of years ago, and we would all be following it and getting the same results. (We'd also be much less sleep-deprived.) Every parent is different, every baby is different, and children are more the products of family and societal dynamics than of one particular style of parenting.

What I can offer you are stories about what our days and nights are like, why we choose to do it this way, and what we see as the benefits for us, our kids, and our community and beyond. I have presented our stories, struggles, and successes in an accessible and simple manner by boiling down all of parenting to five things your baby needs and four things your baby doesn't need (even though people will tell you that they do). Babies need: 1) a smooth birth, 2) food, 3) holding in the day, 4) holding at night (new parents: beware!), and 5) to go potty. Babies don't need: 1) a lot of stuff (frugal parents: rejoice!), 2) unnecessary medical interventions, 3) pressure to achieve too early, and 4) harsh discipline.

Each chapter uses our family's personal experiences and my reflections and perspectives. I will offer you the research, discussions, and benefits that our decisions were based on, as well as where you can go to learn more and make your own informed decisions. I will tell you what we have found surprising, and in some cases, I will share what hasn't worked for us and why. But this is not a parenting book. If it is, it's not like any other parenting book I have read. Parenting books proclaim, "I have figured out how to (fill in the blank as to what you want your baby to do/be/think/feel). Come read this book and you can be just like me!" Parenting books make me feel that I am failing and inadequate since I can't—or won't—get my baby to (fill in the blank again). I guarantee you that I don't know how to raise your kids; I know how to raise mine. This is not a judgmental book. This is not a book in which I explain to you why what you have done or want to do is wrong, and why your children will be forever scarred by your selfish and outrageous parenting. You and your family are the only ones who can decide how to parent.

Finally, this is not about an incredibly difficult or expensive way of life, nor is it a celebrity-telling-you-how-to-live-from-the-privilege-of-luxury-comfort-and-round-the-clock-assistance book. I am sharing my life and my parenting with you simply because I believe in it and I do it every day, every hour, every minute. I do not have housekeepers, nannies, babysitters, extended family, chefs, and personal trainers helping me to be the parent I claim to be. My husband and I are the only caregivers for our kids, and we have no outside help. We have been on three dates in six years, and the only vacations we take are with our kids. We have not been away on a romantic getaway since I was pregnant with our first son, and that wasn't terribly romantic, since I was so pregnant that I practically needed a stretcher to move around . . . and why I thought a maternity *bikini* was a good idea eludes me now.

What worked for our family was for me to complete my degree but not pursue a position in academia, since it did not allow us to parent according to the principles we held true. Returning to acting as I have done since our second son was out of infancy allows me flexible hours, no interruption in nursing our son on demand, nor change in our sleeping arrangements since we travel only as a family unit, and I have the ability to see my children most of the day, even when I am working. My courageous and patient husband completed his master's degree but did not pursue a doctorate, choosing instead to be home with our children so that when I am called to work, our boys' caregiver is their devoted, competent, and loving father.

Parenting using the principles of attachment theory is truly about getting back to basics, valuing the choices you have made, and reaping the benefits of those choices so that you can be present with your kids, loving with your spouse, and content with your life.

As you dive into this book, I implore you to forget what you have been told; forget what the conventional books say. Start with a blank slate, which is actually not very blank at all. It contains billions upon billions of amino acids all lined up and ready to go: your genetic code, your DNA, contains the foundation for every thought, desire, and action you will ever hope to make. The wisdom is there; you just need to learn to trust yourself and unearth your instincts.

I know that most aspects of parenting may not strike you at all as natural or intuitive. After all, what seems natural about propelling an eight-pound baby out of your body? Why would it feel instinctually appropriate to not sleep longer than three hours at a time for years? Read on with an open mind, since incredible introspection can come from such open-mindedness. And when you feel a tug as you are told something by a well-meaning friend, doctor, or stranger that does not sound okay to you, *that* is evidence that your DNA is struggling to be heard above the din of "popular" parenting advice. With the knowledge and support that every parent on this planet deserves, harvesting your intuition won't make being a parent easy; but it can make it meaningful, pleasurable, and life-affirming. The rewards are waiting for us if we follow our intuition.

2

What Is Attachment Parenting?
The Science of Attachment and Intuition

When people hear that I have a PhD in neuroscience, they assume I'm really smart. I like to tell people that I'm not smart, just very persistent. I also let people know that I usually only use the "Dr." title when calling myself Dr. Mom, since the bulk of my time is spent observing, studying, problem-solving, understanding, and loving my two kids. When people learn about my choices in parenting, they either don't associate my degree with my parenting style, or they fear that one needs my level of education to successfully implement this style of parenting. Both are wrong.

I had my first son five years into my doctoral program at UCLA. I had been planning to become a research professor specializing in the role of hormones on obsessive-compulsive disorder in children with special needs, which was the topic of my thesis. However, once I had Miles, my worldview shifted dramatically, and the things I wanted from life revolved around wanting to be with him most of the day, not with a laboratory or classroom full of someone else's kids. What helped me make this very personal decision was the information I learned from studying neuroscience—specifically, developmental neuroscience and the endocrinology of attachment behavior in humans, both of which were required as background for my thesis.

Do you need to be a doctoral candidate in neuroscience to use the concepts of attachment parenting? No—especially since I have already gone ahead and done that for you! My training merely helped me support my decisions with facts and a perspective that has given me a certain degree of confidence. The style of parenting I espouse is not an indulgent way of life for those with a lot of time, money, or a staff of nannies; it is an evolutionarily beneficial commitment that optimizes healthy brain and social development through what is called "secure attachment." Let's learn a little bit in everyday terms about what the brain needs, what babies need, and why the style of parenting our family lives by helps meet those needs easily and successfully.

Brain Development 101

Human beings have brains that are made for loving, cuddling, and secure attachment. Here's why.

Tight squeeze

We are born with underdeveloped brains. This means that over hundreds of thousands of years of evolutionary trial and error, the skills and intelligence we have—the ability to speak and to reason; to love and to memorize and encode complex things like how your beloved grandmother smelled and how smelling her perfume even in a bottle reminds you of the pound cake she made that you loved to eat while sitting perched on her cozy lap—all of this takes up space in the brain. If the brain had to accommodate all of those capabilities at birth, the baby's head would not fit through the vaginal birth canal because the brain would be too big. There is simply not enough room in the newborn brain to hold all of that stuff in its mature form.

Nature has designed it so that a baby is born with a brain that finishes growing in the first year of life, when the baby is outside of the mama. So now you know why it's such a tight squeeze to get the baby's head out of your body: nature has given us the biggest possible head that will eventually accommodate the biggest possible brain. If it were any smaller, we would not be as smart as we are, and if it were any bigger, baby simply wouldn't make it through the birth canal! Thank you, Nature, for making labor a little bit easier, but maybe in another million years contractions can come in the form of sound waves?

The human brain needs love

Sometimes advances in science occur because of very unfortunate and even tragic situations. For example, injuries on the battlefield during the Civil War led to vast improvements in our knowledge of surgery and amputations. An example that is relevant to our understanding of attachment comes out of the harsh political and social climate in Romania over the past thirty years, which led to thousands of babies born to families unable or unwilling to care for them. The result was that tens of thousands of babies and young children were forced into crowded and underfunded orphanages, where they were often left to their own devices to meet their physical and emotional needs. This devastating tragedy led to a secondary one: these children were largely not able to succesfully have their needs met, and they became examples of how the lack of touch, care, and love can lead to children who fail to thrive—they waste away, they become very ill, and they are emotionally traumatized from being denied adequate attention. This trauma is often irreversible.

It would seem intuitive to understand, but this "accidental" experiment (and others' situations like it that can be found in various pockets throughout the world) provides concrete proof that children must have their needs responded to in order to flourish and reach their fullest potential. Although we rarely encounter situations this dire in our daily lives, the infant brain is a sponge for learning all kinds of information; the lessons we teach in the first months and the first years serve as an imprint for all future psychological experiences. Children who are used to being responded to learn that their needs are responded to when they express them, and they learn that using effective communication gets their needs met efficiently and consistently. Children with this knowledge are not spoiled, manipulative, or coddled; rather, they know that they are important to someone who loves them, and they learn to return that kindness through their behavior and their interactions with others.

You may have heard people say that in the first year, a baby's wants and a baby's needs are the same thing. This means that in the first year especially, the things babies indicate they want (usually by crying or "whining" until their language develops further) ought to be considered needs. The easiest ones to understand are the desires or wants to eat and sleep. However, wanting to be held, cuddled, caressed, and cooed to is also a need. These interactions help a baby's brain develop, they establish a healthy concept of reliability and care, and they lay the foundation for a lifetime of expecting good things, asking for them appropriately, and being able to give back when others express *their* needs.

The human brain needs secure attachment

Psychologist John Bowlby defined attachment as the "lasting psychological connectedness between human beings." He noted four things:

1. We want to be physically close to people we are attached to (our "attachment figure" is usually a parent).
2. Exploring the environment occurs when the attachment figure acts as a secure home base.
3. When we are afraid or threatened, we show a desire to return to our attachment figure for safety.
4. We become anxious when we are separated from our attachment figure.

Bowlby studied a lot of children and a lot of parents. He studied families with problematic situations as well as "normal" families. His research led to the identification of four main types of attachment.

Type of Attachment	As children . . .	As adults . . .
Disorganized	Resistant to seeking comfort, acts confused or fearful, has to take care of the parent's emotional needs	Anxiety, depression, developmental problems, dissociative tendencies, "acting out"
Avoidant	Avoids seeking comfort from parents, does not seem to know the difference between comfort from strangers versus comfort from parents	Intimacy problems, problems investing emotionally in relationships, unable to share feelings with others
Ambivalent	Wary of new people, becomes extremely distressed if parent leaves the room, remains distressed and inconsolable when parent returns	Wary of being close to others, excessive worry of being disliked, extreme distress when a relationship ends

Secure	Upset when separated from parent, greets parents positively when they return, seeks comfort from parent when scared, prefers parents over strangers	Trusting, loving relationships, good self-esteem, shares emotions easily with others, seeks social support

In case you hate charts, I will break it down for you this way: disorganized attachment means the child has experienced a lot of trauma, usually as a result of neglect and/or physical abuse, and behaves as if constantly scared. These children often become the caregivers for their parents' needs, and as adults they have trouble connecting with people and may be described as having unresolved issues. Children with avoidant attachment patterns do not go to their parents for comfort because the parents are unable to be that safe place to turn to for comfort. These children do not see much difference between their parents or strangers in terms of needs being met or tended to. As adults, they tend to have relationship and/or intimacy problems, and they don't share their inner thoughts and feelings. Ambivalent attachment means that the child has experienced a fractured relationship with a parent due to the parent's limited resources for handling his or her own life and stresses. These children are tentative, scared of new people, become extremely distressed when the parent leaves the room, and they are unable to be calmed down even when their parent returns. Adults who had ambivalent attachment are afraid to get close to others and experience great distress if relationships do not work out.

Securely attached children separate from their parents easily, react well when reunited with them, seek out their parents for comfort and security, and prefer their parents to strangers. For adults, secure attachment looks like strong healthy relationships and self-esteem, the sharing of emotions, and the pursuit of emotional support when needed. This is the kind of attachment we want to foster in our children.

As you can tell from the styles of attachment that are generally accepted by modern psychology, there is no "spoiled rotten" outcome, nor is there a "manipulative, whiny" outcome. Thinking of children as a reflection of how securely attached they are allows you to peel away the labels and judgments we are given by popular media and parenting books that seek to help you get your child to essentially be a miniature adult who is nonintrusive, obedient, and virtually self-reliant before she can even tie her shoes. What you should realize is that what determines a child's success both in relationships and with themselves is a strong foundation of trust, love, and care. We all want securely attached children, and while independence is a very important quality, so is secure dependence.

The situations that lead to disorganized, ambivalent, and avoidant attachment are not normally seen in an average sampling of children, but they demonstrate how susceptible children are to our own coping mechanisms, our interactions, and our care for them. Attachment parenting promotes secure dependence as the foundation for independence when a child indicates the time is right. Families that don't force independence encourage children to grow at their own pace, fully express their needs, and feel truly understood. This style of parenting is not the *only* way to guarantee a securely attached child, but in my experience and observations, I would hedge my bets that this path, broad though it can be, is a great way toward a smooth and minimally complicated relationship with children.

I repeat: I am not implying that if you do not follow attachment parenting your child will display disorganized, ambivalent, or avoidant attachment. Rather, with this knowledge of the dynamics of attachment, I hope you will be able to see why attachment theory makes sense for what I propose.

Other Scientific Stuff You Oughta Know

We're almost done with the science stuff, I promise. But first we are going to learn a few more terms you have probably heard bandied about but maybe never quite grasped. I will make this as painless as possible.

Hormones

You've probably heard of raging hormones, as in those of a teenager during puberty, or hormone replacement therapy for women in menopause. Maybe you've also heard that steroid drugs are hormones, and that's true, too. Here's the deal: in the middle of your brain, there is a small structure of cells and information superhighways called the hypothalamus. It is attached to the pituitary gland. Together, the hypothalamus and the pituitary gland play a role in almost everything that goes on in your body, including sleep, sexual development and activity, weight gain and loss, thirst, and even your emotional well-being. They also play a huge role in every single aspect of parenting. How do these tiny structures in your brain accomplish this? With hormones.

Hormones are chemicals that are sent out from various places in the brain and throughout the body. They enter your bloodstream and act as messengers to affect you in all sorts of ways. The hormones responsible for everything you think of when you picture having and caring for a baby are all based in two amazing regions of your brain—the hypothalamus and the pituitary gland. Getting and staying pregnant, birth, labor, delivery, nursing, bonding with your baby, feeling attached to him and competent as a parent, and even helping your body return to its prepregnancy state after you have your baby—all of this is regulated by these hormones.

The main hormones important for parenting are oxytocin and vasopressin. Thousands of research studies in hundreds of species of animals (including humans) have confirmed that without the right amounts of oxytocin and vasopressin in your brain and body, getting pregnant, having a safe delivery, nursing effectively, having your uterus return to its prepregnancy size, and wanting to love and care for your baby all become altered, with pretty astonishing results. A healthy experience of parenting—no matter if you are a bird, a rodent, a cat, a chimpanzee, or a human—needs healthy hormones.

Why am I telling you all of this? Because none of it is an accident. Nature has designed our brains and our bodies to parent optimally; that is, to have babies, protect them, nourish them, and perpetuate the species. For example, oxytocin is released when a baby's head pushes against the mother's closed cervix at about forty weeks gestation. Oxytocin causes the uterus to start contracting, thus helping push the baby out of the birth canal and into the world. In addition, nursing a newborn triggers the release of oxytocin, which does two things: it makes the milk release from your breasts, and it causes contractions of your uterus that help it to shrink back to its normal size as quickly as possible. If shrinking does not happen relatively quickly, it can be medically dangerous to the mother. (For this reason, doctors in hospitals will err on the side of caution and administer a synthetic version of oxytocin called Pitocin to a woman when she gives birth, whether she plans to nurse or not.)

Every aspect of being a parent has been essentially programmed and accounted for before humans even appeared on this planet. The "natural" way to get pregnant, have a baby, feed it, and care for it depends on the hormones that all animals share. So don't panic: the hormones are in charge and you are okay!

. . . .

Take-home message

Oxytocin and vasopressin naturally work together in your body to help it have the best possible start on all aspects of parenting.

. . . .

Body/mind connection

It's not just pop psychology or watered-down Eastern philosophy that claims the body and mind are connected. It's neurobiologically accurate. All of the hormones in your body act on the parts of your brain that control emotions, and some hormones even act on physical and emotional aspects of your experiences at the same time. Oxytocin, for example, creates a feeling of emotional satiation and pleasure. How do we know this? Well, since I already told you that oxytocin is responsible for the contraction of muscles, it might not surprise you that, albeit in different amounts and with different areas of activation, oxytocin is the hormone secreted when you experience an orgasm! For the record, nursing and labor do not feel like an orgasm, but there are aspects that are very pleasant, and nature wants it that way so that you continue to nourish your baby and have more of them! Oxytocin is also the hormone responsible for helping us experience the feeling of trust, which is a very important thing to feel both in labor and when you are connecting sexually to someone with the possibility that you will be getting pregnant and carrying those genes into the next generation. I repeat: none of this is an accident! Nature has made great use of hormones to help you physically be capable of parenting and to experience emotions that are crucial to being a good parent.

. . . .

Take-home message

Hormones are necessary for our bodies and minds to function well.

. . . .

Intuition

Now that you are a sort of expert in how hormones are important for the physical as well as emotional aspects of parenting, it should not come as a surprise to you that intuition and instinct are not made-up concepts. They are the result of the chemicals in your brain and body that tell you what to do and how to act. It's intuitive!

The concept of having an intuitive knowledge about being a parent is based on how our DNA is programmed and designed. Many modern parents have been encouraged to rely on medical professionals to guide them in their decisions about being parents. I believe, and I hope you will come to believe as well, that we intuitively know how to interpret an infant's cries and signals; we know how to give birth and what feels right while we are in labor; *we know how to be parents*. It is our birthright since the dawn of our species to have ownership of our intuition, which I think makes for an easier time learning your baby's signals, caring for your baby, and enjoying being a parent. Why fight nature and all of those hormones?

. . . .

Take-home message

It's your evolutionary right to tap in to your intuition to enjoy every stage of parenthood. You were made to be a parent!

. . . .

What Is Missing?

You may have noticed that with everything I have said thus far about the science behind parenting, I have left out three words that anyone who has read a conventional parenting book has seen dozens of times. These three words are: schedule, training, and independence. Here's why I left them out.

1. Babies don't need schedules; parents do.

To a newborn, there is no such thing as a schedule. Newborn babies have no concept of day or night, nor do they give a good gosh darn if you are tired, grumpy, premenstrual, upset about the latest breakup on your favorite soap opera, whatever. They have no schedule because they don't need one. As I said before, their wants are their needs for at least the first year of life. This means that if they *want* to nurse, they *need* to nurse. If they *want* to sleep, they *need* to sleep. And if they *want* to be held, they *need* to be held. This may sound daunting and draining, and it is. But it also makes a lot of sense, and I think you will be spared a lot of drama if you try to roll with it and see the rewards, which are highlighted particularly in chapter 6 on nighttime parenting.

2. Babies don't need to be trained.

Many people choose to train babies because they are told that the baby needs them too much, is manipulating them, is too clingy, and so on. Training is something parents are told to do when they don't know what else to do. Parenting counselors, pediatricians, nurses, and family and friends love suggesting that you "sleep train" or "condition" your baby to not *need* you so much, but as you will see, parenting by your natural intuition allows you to put a whole new spin on your concept of what babies crave and how to make that happen so that everyone is happy (and maybe even rested).

3. Our culture values independence at a shockingly early age compared with much of the world and with other primates.

Parents are often told that their infant should be sleeping through the night, should be self-soothing, and should really stop being so needy by a few months old. (This advice astounds me even when I hear it regarding a six-, nine-, or even twelve- or eighteen-month-old!) Our culture values babies who sit up on their own (and can thus theoretically entertain themselves—ha!), babies who speak early (so that they can express themselves clearly, we are told, without the "frustration" of us not understanding them—or having to stay close to them to learn their cues, is more like it), and babies who are quiet (crying and loud vocalizing are generally discouraged and are even cause for harsh discipline in some circles). We all want independent children. The question of when that independence must emerge varies, but the assumption that independent children can come only from independent babies is not only scientifically unproven, it's silly. The style of parenting that works for us and for so many parents trusts that you know your child better than anyone. Healthy dependence in the early years can and does breed healthy independence later on.

How to Start Your Parenting Journey

Priorities, priorities

This is going to sound really cliché, but I am going to say it anyway: what do you want written on your tombstone? How's this: "Here lies so-and-so. Devoted employee, excellent typist, very organized and task-oriented. People person, lived to earn money, and died at a desk full of completed reports." Doesn't sound so appealing, does it?

I won't tell you what *I* think your tombstone should say, but I will guarantee you that how you live your life is what you will leave as your legacy. Being a present and devoted parent is more meaningful and important than anything in this world, and I don't say that from a place of self-righteousness. Choosing to be involved with your child is a gift above gifts, and we all want our children to become adults who want to spend time with us, seek our advice, and respect us. We need to be there for them early on to have the best chance at this outcome.

Does this mean you can be a good parent only if you are an at-home parent? Not at all. Does it mean you should homeschool your children so that you spend every possible second of your time with them? No. I simply implore you—at whatever stage of parenting you find yourself when you read this—to look into your heart, ignore the voice in your head telling you why you shouldn't listen, and discover what your intuition tells you about what kind of parent you want to be. If you already have children, do they need more of you than you want them to need? Do you feel guilty when you are not attentive to their needs, and do you keep brushing off that guilty feeling, saying to them or yourself, "Someone has to pay the bills!" Are you the parent you want to be? If you are not yet a parent, what do you see as the ideal for the parent you want to be?

There is time enough for achieving financial success, accolades, and "getting ahead" besides the first years of your child's life. To parent by intuition means to listen first and foremost to your family's needs and adjust your life around those needs, not the other way around. I so often hear couples tell me that they both "have to" work. While this is sometimes true, these same couples who tell me how they wish they could just stay at home with their kids sometimes make decisions to live in trendy and expensive parts of expensive cities, buy expensive cars, and take expensive vacations. I am not knocking people who want to live this way, but those are examples of things many people choose not to do so that one parent can stay home with their kids. Plenty of people make drastic changes to their living situations and go without a lot of niceties because they believe more fervently in the value of being home with their children. Not everyone wants to, but for many people, it is a priority worth adjusting to accommodate.

Never before in your life has prioritizing been as important as it is when you are a parent. You will never get back the chance to give your child the first years of life. All of the psychological imprinting that goes on, all of the patterns they experience, the rhythms they move to, and the feelings they have even before they can speak, these are what makes your children the people they will be at five, ten, and even at fifteen, twenty-five, and thirty-five. There are so many more resources now than there ever have been for people to get help and support to be the parents they want to be. Don't regret it later. Decide what your priorities are now and make them happen.

Realistic expectations

One of the main things that I wish I had known before I had my first son was that I needed to better understand what it means to set, and be comfortable with, realistic expectations.

When you become a parent, there's a physical component of realistic expectations: you will never accomplish in a day what you did before you became a parent. You may never again cook a three-course meal in an hour, and it may be a long time before you even eat an entire meal sitting down again. For a very long time you will not go to the cleaners, the supermarket, get your hair done, get the car washed, pick up your favorite little Moroccan appetizers from that cute little café near your house and get home in time to put a casserole in the oven, take a hot bath, and be ready to serve your spouse dinner before a night of mind-blowing sex followed by sleeping in and playing tennis after a champagne brunch at the country club. (I'm giggling just thinking about this whole ridiculous, decadent scenario!) Visiting the bathroom will often be done as an afterthought, and you will be amazed at how long you can wait to pee after first realizing you have to. I have often had this kind of dialogue with myself: *I'll go to the bathroom before we leave the house. Oops, I forgot to go. I'll go when we get to the park. Oops, I forgot. I'll go at the restaurant. Oops, there was too much food flying through the air for me to remember to go. I'll go when I get home. Oops, my husband's not home. I'll go when he comes home* (thirty minutes later). *Okay, he's home, I can go. Oh, he has to go, too? I'll go after he goes.* And so on.

Then there is an emotional component of realistic expectations: Now that you are a parent, your brain simply cannot contain what it used to. Friendships are not as easily maintained, especially in the first months of your baby's life. The things you used to do to de-stress (gym, massage, long walks by the lake) cannot be done with the same frequency as they were before. You will constantly feel pulled in a million directions, and you can barely focus on current events, much less how to go back to work or have an adult conversation without the word "poop" in it. You may feel for the first time that you simply *cannot do this*. All normal.

I guarantee you that it won't feel this way forever. Situations and your emotional reaction to them will shift every day, sometimes every hour, sometimes more frequently than that. As they shift, I implore you not to fight it. Don't beat yourself up for being less productive than you once were. It will only lead to more exhaustion and feelings of incompetence and defeat. Don't fight the waves; try to see their movement as an embrace. There are ways to make simple adjustments to your life that can lessen this tension (see chapter 13 on balance). It's all going to be okay, as long as you know you are not who you once were and you are doing the best that you can. And there are people who can help you feel empowered, supported, and justified in your choices. You will find that reasonable and realistic lowered expectations can really be quite liberating!

Learn to smile at annoying people

There's no elegant way to say this: when you have a baby, you get to see how utterly annoying a lot of people are. Everyone has an opinion on what you are doing or not doing; everyone knows some isolated case of a kid who suffered a horrible tragedy because his parents did "exactly what you're doing"; everyone feels the need to defend the way they were parented or the way they are parenting by undermining your choices; and everyone is an expert on your kid. These annoying people are allowed their opinions, but you don't have to agree with them.

I learned this the hard way.

With my first son, I wanted to please everyone and explain myself and defend my choices, but the truth was that most people didn't want to hear my reasons, my research, or our pediatrician's credentials. They simply wanted to be right. Other people's opinions can make you insane as a parent, and I recommend that you master the art of smiling, taking a deep breath, thinking happy thoughts for the annoying person in your face, and politely excusing yourself to the bathroom. You don't need to be right; you simply need to be the best parent you can be. And *you* are the best authority on your child; no one else is.

I am writing this book to help you build the confidence I did not have early on so that you can trust your intuition more than you might right now. You deserve and have the right to set boundaries; it will be a critical skill for you as a parent, so start now with all of the people you meet who give you unsolicited advice. Practice saying into the mirror, with a smile plastered on your serene face, "Thanks for your opinion. I'll give it some thought. Talk to you later, I have to go to the bathroom!"

Take it slow

For thousands of years, traditional cultures have instituted a forty day or so adjustment period for a new mother. This practice, sometimes known as a "lying-in period," often correlates with the amount of time a woman's body typically takes to recover from a birth, but it also protects a new mother from returning too soon to the daily grind and allows her to focus her energy and resources on her baby while being showered with attention, food, and care from her community. Many modern parents are choosing to reinstate this practice, and I cannot recommend it highly enough, even in an abbreviated or modified form.

Consistent with everything I have indicated about you not being able to accomplish with a newborn what you could accomplish without one, an adjustment period (even of a week) forces you to adjust to a new pace of life. It allows you to observe your baby without the challenges of socializing too much, risking exhaustion or injury to your healing body, or distracting yourself from the task at hand, which is to learn to love and nourish this tiny, fragile, and totally incomprehensible miracle in your arms.

If this sounds impossible and you are already imagining the things you need to do once a baby is born, that's all the more reason why you should do it. Some people do "seven days *in* the bed, seven days *on* the bed, seven days *around* the bed," which is exactly what it sounds like. Others do a full forty days (this comes out to six weeks, which is when your postpartum checkup will most likely be), and some people do what they can, reaching enough outside of their comfort zone to see what their new life will be like and growing from there.

Whatever you choose, know that having a child is absolutely wondrous and terrifying at the same time. In many ways, *you* feel like the newborn: you are flailing, unprepared, without the vocabulary to express your needs, and badly in need of a bath. Your life as you knew it has ended, and this new one is not exactly a vacation in Hawai'i. Be gentle with yourself, and give yourself the gift of slowing down. It's good for you, it's good for the baby, and it will make your transition from no baby to baby a little bit smoother. And, by the way, you can and should do this with baby #2, #3, and so on. It may not look exactly the same, but you can still have the intent and allow adjustment to work its magic.

Ready?

You now have some scientific background to help you understand why attachment parenting makes sense evolutionarily. I have told you about secure attachment and the hormones of your body and mind and how they help you know organically what being a parent should look like. I have also given you some tips to prepare you for your journey. So hang on to your hats and glasses—it's going to be a wild ride!

Part II

What Baby Needs

3

Baby Needs a Smooth Entrance: Birth

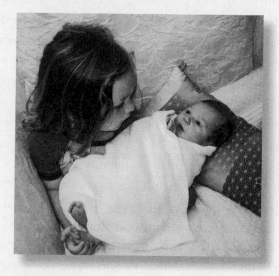

Picture yourself an animal in the wild. Any mammal will do: a lion, a gazelle, maybe a bear. Or go crazy and pick a "cousin" of yours: a primate; perhaps a chimpanzee?

Okay, so you're in the wild and you are pregnant. What does it look like when it's time to give birth? Well, there are no doctors checking you for dilation or cervical softening, no fetal monitors, no stripping of your membranes to initiate labor, and no real concept of a due date. As a mammal, in the final weeks of your pregnancy, you experience a spontaneous surge of hormones that encourage you to stay close to "home." Labor typically begins at night, in the darkness, when the hormone oxytocin (which encourages labor) is at its peak. You steal away from the rest of your family and community and find a quiet, safe place to labor. You are alone but you are not scared.

You do not receive anesthesia or opiates, and your baby emerges with no one holding your legs up or encouraging you to lie horizontally. In addition, no one shouts at you to push; you just listen to your body and push when it becomes clear that there is nothing else to do. You examine your newborn and eat the high-protein placenta around your baby, and then you nurse. No one washes the baby off, smears cream in the baby's eyes, or injects the baby with anything. You return to your family and friends and rest with your baby.

Congratulations: you have just birthed, guided by the primal and evolutionarily ancient part of your brain! It's the same part of your brain that operates during really satisfying, amazing sex. When the primal brain is at work, it doesn't care what the temperature is in the south of France, what designer this year's Academy Award–winning actress wore on the red carpet, or what the cost of a loaf of bread is at the local supermarket. You don't need intellect to have awesome sex, and you don't need intellect to give birth; you need the primal brain that cannot hold down a sensible, coherent conversation but can sure as heck accomplish what it needs to do to perpetuate the species.

If you are a human in the United States, labor and birth tend to look very different from that of our mammalian relatives. Pregnancy is typically seen as a medical condition to be managed (most women even insist that a doctor's test "confirm" that they are pregnant!), and labor is more and more often being induced when busy doctors and eager mothers decide they are done being pregnant. In the name of efficiency, these often fear-filled doctors decide they are not comfortable waiting for labor to begin naturally. The United States boasts a C-section rate that is among the highest in the world, hovering around 30 percent, when the World Health Organization recommends it stay closer to 15 percent for the safety of both babies and their mothers. In fact, when a country's cesarean-section rate rises above 15 percent, the dangers of the surgery actually outweigh the benefits it supposedly provides.

Lest you assume that all of these technological interventions have been better for babies, note that many developed countries have a better infant survival rate than the United States, which ranks only forty-third out of 196 countries, according to the United Nations. And these technological interventions are not necessarily better for mothers, either—the outcomes for mothers are usually better in countries that practice fewer interventions in labor and birth. In the United States, white women have a mortality rate of 9.5 per 100,000 pregnancies, and African-American women have a mortality rate of 32.7 per 100,000 pregnancies, according to the CDC. As a point of reference, the countries with the lowest infant and maternal mortality rates are countries that employ midwives as primary caregivers for births, encourage natural birth, and make home birth comfortable and available to all women who are not contraindicated for it: Sweden, Denmark, and Norway. These countries also offer paid maternity leave for a full year with an option of half pay for the second year, so call the immigration office now to find out how soon you can move there.

Problems with Unnecessary Interventions

In some cases, interventions are necessary and useful in labor. However, the use of unnecessary interventions that are done preemptively to "protect" the mother are *not* benign, nor are they always safe for mama and baby. Unnecessary interventions increase the likelihood of a variety of complications that would not be present if the intervention had not been introduced, so many births end up with what is called the "snowball effect": intervention-induced complications lead to further interventions, and so on . . .

What is most disturbing about the interventions that are used to start, help along, and end labor and birth, though, is that they interfere with both our intuition and our body's instincts. For example, interventions that are used to start labor are sometimes recommended because it has been deemed that the woman's body does not know how (or when) to go into labor, a process that is governed by powerful hormones and musculature, and that has been refined over hundreds of thousands of years of evolution. The notion that the mammalian body needs help starting labor is, to be quite frank, kind of disturbing. It is only in an environment where women are trained to not listen to their bodies, or when their emotional health and security is tampered with, that distrust in ourselves reigns and we turn outward for reassurance and guidance about what is natural to us.

In the early stages of my first labor, I was having contractions slowly and steadily, but our doctor wanted them closer together. He wanted to move things along and stated the following: "If I induce you, you will probably end up with a C-section." This caused my adrenaline to shoot through the roof, and my contractions literally stopped after I left his office. I was, to put it simply, scared out of labor. This frequently happens to women; we are told we are not progressing fast enough, and lo and behold: we stop progressing at all.

That most women carry a baby for forty weeks is helpful information, but the fact that due dates are based on menstrual cycles and rarely on actual conception dates leaves room for error, since a few days either way can make a huge difference when your choices are to be induced or to allow your body to begin labor on its own. There are even reports that women who use in vitro fertilization (IVF) have longer gestation periods in general, so these women may need a longer window of time in which to start labor before it is assumed they will never go into labor!

The most common interventions used in labor and delivery are:

Pitocin: A synthetic hormone injected into your bloodstream that stimulates contractions. Pitocin is given both to speed up labor that is not progressing as fast as it "should be" and it is also used to induce labor, if a doctor determines that you should be in labor but your body has not initiated this process on its own yet. Pitocin is also used after the baby is born, in order to encourage the uterus to contract and expel the placenta, a process that in a natural birth the body can typically handle without the administration of this drug. In higher doses, Pitocin can be given to help stop hemorrhaging, if it occurs. (Baby's sucking at the breast brings in natural oxytocin.)

Epidural: An injection of anesthesia into the space between your skin and your spinal cord to numb the nerves below the site of injection that communicate information about sensation and pain to your brain. This injection typically requires continuous drip of saline (fluid) for the entire course of time you receive the epidural, as epidurals need to be readministered roughly every two to three hours.

Drugs: Throughout the history of hospital birth, women have been given a variety of drugs, including narcotics and tranquilizers, for pain and "emotional" management during labor and delivery.

Vacuum extraction: When the pushing stage of labor is determined not to be progressing, a suction cup is placed onto the baby's head and attached to a device that quite literally vacuums the baby out of the mother's body.

Forceps: In cases where the baby is perceived to be stuck or pushing is not progressing, a large pair of tongs is placed around the baby's head inside of your vagina and the baby is pulled out of your body. This practice has lost favor as C-sections and vacuum extraction have gained popularity.

Episiotomy: An incision between the perineum and the posterior vaginal wall. Some emergency situations warrant episiotomy, but routine episiotomy has become popular when labor is not progressing as fast as desired. Episiotomy was also purported to prevent tearing of the perineum, a claim that is currently unsubstantiated. The practice of routine episiotomy has been declared unnecessary by the American Congress of Obstetricians and Gynecologists and is recognized as useful only in specific acute emergency situations.

Cesarean Section: A major surgical procedure in which incisions are made in a woman's abdomen and uterus to deliver a baby. C-sections require anesthesia, narcotics for pain management, and an intense healing process, with limited movement and mobility, during which your ability to care for yourself and your newborn will be significantly impaired.

Many women feel pressure to have a C-section because their doctors tell them that the baby is "too big." Sadly, in a society that values thin over all else, many women may actually not mind hearing, "You're too petite to deliver this baby." But once again, our bodies were made to deliver our babies. Our bodies were designed with enough room for our babies to make it through the passageway. There is innate knowledge that has been programmed into our DNA, and we were designed to birth babies with large heads (the better to grow a large brain in!). The primate baby's head houses the brain—the organ of cognition, speech, and reasoning. And the primate head was designed with soft and malleable skeletal plates that solidify only once the baby is out of your body, so as to allow the baby to squeeze through the birth canal (and it feels like a tight squeeze because it is!) with a large skull intact—and with the mother intact as well. The thought of a baby getting stuck in the birth canal is terrifying, but it ought not be used as a threat; women should not be scared of birthing vaginally—it's the way nature intended it.

An aside about vaginal birth after cesarean (VBAC): it was previously thought that women who had delivered a baby by C-section risked a rupture of the uterus if a subsequent birth was attempted vaginally, estimated at anywhere from 0.2 to 1.5 percent, which is less than one in five hundred women. Sophisticated statistics have recently revealed that rupture rates are highest for women whose labors were induced by Pitocin; the powerful drugs of induction are apparently playing a role in the rupture rates. In this way, the fear of rupture should actually be a fear not of a VBAC but of an induction!

In 2010, the American Congress of Obstetricians and Gynecologists stated the following: "Attempting VBAC is a safe and appropriate choice for most women who have had a prior cesarean delivery, including for some women who have had two previous cesareans." Women who achieve successful and gratifying VBACs report that they feel empowered and inspired by their body's ability to trust and be trusted to deliver their babies the way they want to, the way nature intended them to.

The VBAC community has been at the forefront of drawing significant attention to the fact that the mother's experience during labor counts and has an impact on the baby beyond which part of her body the baby comes out of. This underscores a very important point about birth that attachment parenting holds sacred: it's not just about how the baby comes out. It's about the experience of labor and delivery for the mother, the baby, and the entire family. It's about feeling competent and capable, because when you feel your decisions and your body are not yours, it does not feel helpful or encouraging. For some women, it can lead to postpartum depression, anxiety, and general doubts about their abilities as a parent.

Even if you have a C-section, your experience still matters and is valuable. The true beauty of attachment parenting's emphasis on birth is to know your choices, to have appropriate expectations about your labor and birth, and to feel empowered within a powerful system of medical mazes. A dear friend of mine prepared for a natural birth using hypnosis and ended up with a C-section. She was emotionally present throughout the whole experience and practiced hypnosis during the procedure with devotion, love, and focus. She wished she could have had a natural, vaginal birth, but she also accepted her situation with the skills she learned, and this is a wonderful thing to remember: the complete birth experience, start to finish, is about getting a healthy baby in your arms. You get to do your part and prepare, and then you get to see what the Universe has in mind!

How to Enjoy a Natural Birth and Avoid Unnecessary Interventions

If you wanted to climb Mount Everest, what would you do? You would probably find someone who knows about Mount Everest, maybe someone who has climbed it, if only once, and you would ask what it was like. You would spend some time with her and find out what it was about her personality that made her able to achieve this incredible feat. Perhaps you would talk to more than one person, and you would find out what she did that was the same as what the others did or what they did that was different. Some questions you might ask would be: What can I do to prepare for this climb? What skills will I need? What classes should I take? What special equipment do I need? What food should I bring along and what first-aid kit? What kinds of emotional and psychological tools do I need to hone and perfect so that I don't give up or feel like I am going crazy when I feel like quitting? Who should I take on my climb and why? Natural birth without any interventions or medication is sort of like climbing Mount Everest.

Many women feel the following way about natural birth: "I'm going to give it a shot, but if I *really* can't stand it, I'm going to take the drugs; that's what they're there for." It is a staggering disservice to women to be told to "try" having a natural birth but be given insufficient resources, education, and support to make it happen. Natural birth is not something you *try;* it's something you learn about, prepare for, and succeed at by completing it. It's something you feel amazing about afterward, and you will feel like . . . well, you will feel like you just climbed Mount Everest!

Here are the things I recommend from experience that give you the best opportunity for a meaningful, smooth, and satisfying natural birth.

Get classy

Not all birth classes are created equal. Attend a birth class *designed for women who want natural labor.* It is great when partners are involved in this process, especially if they are not educated about the benefits and beauty of natural birth, but if they are not interested, it is better for you to go alone to this kind of class than to choose a class to appease your partner. Why? Because you are the one facing the challenges of labor, and you are the one choosing how to get the baby out! The idea is to tap in to your intuition and learn to birth from the inside out: building up your strength, endurance, and knowledge internally so that you can transfer it to the external experience of actual labor. You need a class that doesn't simply pay lip service to natural labor while equating it with medicated labor. By definition, they are not the same thing and should not be treated as such. It's not helpful for you to plan for a natural birth while being told how medicated births are also fantastic. If you wanted to avoid eating meat, would you opt to go to a steak house when you are starving? It's the same concept: put yourself where you want to be and you will find yourself there!

Get read-y

One of the most powerful things I did to prepare for both of my labors was to read autobiographical birth stories of everyday women who had birthed naturally. Especially after my first labor, which did not go as I intended it to, I needed a boost of confidence and faith that only hearing from other women could provide. For all of mothering history, women have learned from their mothers, aunts, sisters, and close friends what labor and birth are like. It's not all sunshine and roses. The goal is not to read about women who didn't feel pain, or women who had superhuman strength. We women are all so different; we have different pain tolerances, different worldviews, different ways we handle challenges. But after giving birth, we are all the same: we are mothers. It is the sharing of the details of labor and birth—the feelings, the sensations, the mantras, musings, and meditations to manage the feelings and the sensations, the ecstasy and the conflict we feel when that baby slides out—that makes you feel part of a community, part of something larger than just your womb. It is this sisterhood that will keep you inspired during labor. I can guarantee it. See the Resources section for specific suggestions.

Get plugged in

Ricki Lake and Abby Epstein's groundbreaking documentary, *The Business of Being Born*, has brought the politics of medicated birth and beauty of natural birth to the public in a way that only technology has made possible. I implore you to rent it, even if you think you have already decided whether to have a natural birth. It will help every mother no matter what she decides. There are numerous other, less publicized documentaries that show beautiful normal births, both at home and in hospital settings (see the Resources section). None of these videos is meant to scare or shock you; they depict real women following their bodies' instincts to birth safely and naturally. My husband was not at all interested in watching any such documentaries, but he ended up fascinated by the presentation and the message even more than by the birth class we took.

Get a doula

A doula is a certified accredited labor coach. She's not your life partner or lover, and you don't want her to be. There are many things your partner can and will do for you during labor, and a doula does not take the place of a spouse. But for all of history (besides the past two hundred years or so), women have helped women birth, and there is a support a trained labor coach can provide that many partners can—and should—not. Labors can proceed more slowly when your adrenaline is higher than it ought to be, and a partner hovering over you can make your adrenaline go through the roof. This is not only because of the observation factor but also because of the complex emotional and psychological relationships we establish with our partners; expectations, preconceived perceptions about behavior and support, and even unresolved conflicts can unconsciously find their way into your brain during labor, and these can sometimes get transferred right to your cervix, causing it to close when you want it to open!

A doula is your personalized support system. She can facilitate hypnosis and relaxation and, if necessary, allow your spouse to rest so that they can be fully present with you the way you need them to be during labor. Doulas operate in hospitals as well as in homes, and they are there to support you, whatever your plans are for birth. Doulas can help you prepare a birth plan/wish list, an extremely critical document for anyone in labor—at home or not, natural labor or not—that puts in writing your desires for labor and birth (see the Resources section for sample birth wish-list worksheet).

Hiring a doula is a wise and worthwhile investment in your plans for birth, since women who employ a doula report significantly lower rates of intervention and reports of pain and fewer unwanted C-sections. Doula fees vary from hundreds to thousands of dollars, with some offering professional photography, your birth story written up, acupuncture, and postpartum assistance and checkups as added features to standard doula services. A woman does not need to have given birth to be an excellent doula, so keep an open mind, and remember that doulas in training are still skilled and sought after, often offering reduced fees since they are gathering hours toward certification.

Get medical

When selecting an obstetrician (OB), ask about his/her C-section rates and attitudes about women who go past their due dates. Be specific and ask everything you need to ascertain an OB's attitude about the female body and its natural ability to give birth. Don't hear what you want to hear: listen objectively to what the doctors are communicating. Listen to how they react to your questions and concerns, *because that is exactly how they will react to your questions and concerns in labor.* Find out what regulations your OB and birthing facility have regarding the necessity of fetal monitors (which tend to limit freedom of movement), and inspect birthing rooms. Are there open showers or tubs to use during labor? Remember that mammals and women are made to give birth smoothly and peacefully and in dark, safe places with minimal observation and interruption. To that end, does your birthing environment have any natural lighting available? Are there windows? A friend of mine rejected a hospital (justifiably, in my opinion) because the birthing rooms had no windows. She said it felt like she would be giving birth in a prison—fair enough. Does the facility have birthing bars to lean on during labor or birthing balls to bounce on to relieve pain? There should be some feeling of "home" wherever you give birth, however you define that or make it happen. These are the "small" details that many people don't think much about that can truly make all the difference for your birth. And again: have a filled-out birth wish list in hand to have your desires in writing.

Get selectively social

If you are pregnant, don't listen to people's negative stories about women who did not succeed at natural births or, worse yet, women who lost babies in labor. Find a sentence to repeat that makes people stop telling you their stories. I suggest: "Thank you so much for wanting to share, but I'm not able to listen at the moment/I don't want to hear it/I'm really sensitive right now to birth stories/I need to go wash my car." Learn to say no and expect it to be honored. You will need this skill as a mother more times than you care to imagine in the first year of your baby's life, when people give you unsolicited advice about how and why and when and where to feed the baby, wondering why you are wearing your baby so much, holding him so much, loving him so much—you get the idea. Talk to women who have had natural birth experiences with positive outcomes. In general, women who have had natural births understand the importance of *not* scaring other women. So if you have a friend who has a friend who is a crunchy-granola woman (like me), ask your friend to be connected to that crunchy-granola woman and talk to her about her positive birth experience. Find out what worked for her, what didn't, what sounds she made during labor, what the sensations were like, what pushing was like, what her partner did or didn't do, how it felt when the baby came out, and how she feels about it now. You get one chance per baby to rock out a natural labor, so do everything you can to make it happen—create the sisterhood!

Get proactive

It's up to you to seek out the resources of organizations that value and support natural birth. This is how you empower yourself and build a support system of women who can help you in this journey. La Leche League International is a breastfeeding organization that places tremendous value and importance on women deciding for themselves what works for them throughout the parenting journey. They hold friendly and fun meetings that are always open to pregnant women. Whenever I attend meetings, we welcome pregnant women to listen to our breastfeeding stories, but embedded in these stories is a faith and trust in our bodies and our decisions. The Holistic Moms Network is another excellent resource for pregnant women. Every meeting and every group is different, but you will undoubtedly find a fantastic network of people who will help you travel this journey with confidence.

Get real

Women (and men) often ask me about the pain of childbirth. Here's my general statement: you do not need to be Superwoman to have a natural labor that you do not later (or during) associate with pain and suffering. Labor is not painful or fear-inducing; rather, labor is intense and requires a tremendous amount of physical and mental focus and energy. The tools available to women who choose natural birth include some of the above suggestions, such as hiring a doula and choosing an OB and birthing environment that value and trust natural birth. But perhaps the single most important thing you can do to manage fear about pain is to learn a new framework for your understanding and experience of pain. It may sound daunting, but it's not. Plenty of non-hippie-dippie regular everyday women achieve this through techniques such as self-hypnosis and deep relaxation and meditation. It doesn't mean you have to become a sufi or a mystic; there are many inexpensive (even free) and simple ways to tap in to your mind's natural ability to shift the processing of pain.

As a neuroscientist, I can explain how this works neurologically, but it's not necessary. Trust that you can totally alter the way you interpret and experience the sensations of labor. You can give birth without suffering, without fear, and without regret. I will let my birth stories do the talking.

My Experience

During the last month of my first pregnancy, I used a self-hypnosis program. I listened to the program's CDs on headphones every night before bed and also once in the day. Besides instruction in self-hypnosis, each CD also featured a guided relaxation that focused on birth and labor expectations, as well as affirmations about the body's intuitive nature and intelligence. Hypnosis is basically teaching yourself deep relaxation, and the affirmations and tools you learn help you to manage pain and breathe through the intensity of "surges" (the kinder, gentler term for contractions).

My first son was two weeks "late" by our backup OB's calculations. I had an uneventful, if large, weight-gaining pregnancy and was planning a home birth with a licensed midwife who was also trained as an emergency nurse and had been birthing babies for almost forty years. I had gestational diabetes (diabetes-like metabolism and blood sugar levels that present in 2 to 10 percent of pregnancies and typically disappear after the baby is born), for which a backup OB has the right and authority to encourage induction should he/she think it is recommended. I decided, with our OB and midwife's support, to try natural induction techniques to get labor moving, since, in my OB's words, if I did not go into labor, he was going to induce me and I would "probably end up with a C-section," which was very far from my desire to birth naturally at home.

I used three natural induction techniques in my early attempts to get labor started. First, I used a variety of midwife and homeopathic physician recommended remedies designed to encourage contractions of the uterus to begin in order to "expel" the baby. Second, I had a few sessions of acupuncture specifically designed to stimulate labor, performed by a skilled and experienced licensed acupuncturist knowledgeable in using acupuncture during pregnancy. Third, I tried moxibustion. This consists of a cigar-like shape of a charcoal-like material (the moxa stick) held over the belly in an attempt to stimulate movement of the fetus down toward the cervix.

The more "aggressive" induction techniques were the use of a breast pump and castor oil to start labor. Since the stimulation of oxytocin encourages uterine contractions and thus gets and keeps labor moving, stimulating the breasts (with a pump or manually, actually, if you want to get technical) encourages the flow of oxytocin and was pretty effective in causing contractions! (I used a pump so much during my days of labor that I actually began to express colostrum, the earliest milk your body produces when your newborn latches on.) Ingesting castor oil is pretty gnarly, but it causes contractions of the rectal and uterine muscles which, again, encourage labor. It tastes really gross and its consistency is extremely . . . oily, and the smell of anything remotely similar to castor oil, even almost seven years after I had to drink it, conjures up memories of labor and birth. It's potent, to say the least.

My water partially broke on a Friday morning and I used my breast pump to keep contractions going for the better part of that weekend. I used self-hypnosis with my doula's guidance and supervision for every single surge, allowing my body to breathe and float through the intensity of surges that felt like the worst menstrual cramps ever, times about fifty. FYI, the intensity was much more mental than physical. By that I mean it wasn't simply the actual physical sensations that felt so intense, it was the mental energy it took to remember that this was normal and I was okay, and if I just kept breathing and didn't panic, each surge would end and I would get a break. It also helped to remember that each surge was helping me move toward meeting my baby—it was going to be all right.

By Monday morning, with no baby and no progress beyond nine centimeters, we made a nonemergency decision to transport me to the hospital. My husband drove me (dilated at nine centimeters, practicing my self-hypnosis the whole way) through the hills of Hollywood to the hospital where my doula and midwife assured the triage nurse that I just needed a room and a little shot of Pitocin because I was "almost done." I labored through the car ride, using my self-hypnosis techniques to go "limp and loose" and block out the sensations of intensity that rose and fell every few minutes. I continued this practice down the hallways of the hospital, leaning quietly against whatever wall was in front of me when a contraction hit, and once given a room, I was then strapped to a monitor, immobile on a hospital bed with an IV in my arm and a very nice nurse who had never witnessed an unmedicated birth. My doula had our birth wish list with her and gently but firmly told the nurses not to even ask me if I desired pain medication. A small dose of Pitocin allowed me to reach ten centimeters quickly, and after one and a half hours of pushing and almost four days since my water broke, I delivered an almost eight-and-a-half-pound healthy boy.

Baby boy Bialik had low blood sugar, a low heart rate, and a low body temperature, which flagged him as a possible case of sepsis or E. coli, we were told. He was whisked away hours after he was born, kicking and screaming, to the neonatal intensive care unit (NICU), where he was placed in an incubator and had testing done ad nauseum. This blew out his veins and caused tremendous distress for us all. I was not permitted to nurse him for two days, but I refused the use of pacifiers or formula for him, despite being told by a NICU pediatric physician that formula was "really no different from nursing." For four days we sat vigil for our giant healthy baby (by NICU standards), and I pumped every two hours for him, even when the hospital discharged me and we were forced to stay in a hotel. The doctors found nothing wrong with our son that could justify his being there, so they simply sent us home. Since then, he has never had any problems with his heart, blood sugar, or body temperature, nor has he ever even been on antibiotics.

That's the short story. The hospital experience turned out as well as I could have hoped, minus the NICU part. My birth team helped me have the closest second option for me: a vaginal birth in a hospital with no pain medication. Our OB tried to make me feel better by explaining that some women's bodies just don't know when to start labor. I cringed and shrank at the thought that I might have been left behind in evolution's survival of the fittest were it not for medical intervention.

My second pregnancy was healthier overall, and I had no

diabetes, although I ate as if I did just to be safe. The baby and I proved our OB wrong, and we began labor one day after his due date at 5:30 a.m. By 8:30 that morning I had pushed him out.

Labor went significantly faster than anyone anticipated, and I labored through all ten centimeters by myself, pacing and rocking on all fours, staring out the front door, chanting psalms and mantras to myself. The part of my brain that had been told by our culture to be scared kept trying to take over: What if no one comes? What if there's a problem? What do I do next? But I kept forcing myself to dip into the knowledge that my doula and midwives and hypnosis affirmations and so many women whose stories I had re-read the night before gave me: I can do this. My body knows how to birth my baby. I was made to birth my baby. The techniques of self-hypnosis I used in my first labor weren't as necessary for me in this one, since my body told me to keep moving. I listened to my body: When it needed to move, I moved. When I needed to vocalize, I did. And when I needed to pray, I prayed. The principles of those hypnosis CDs and the positive affirmations that were drilled into my head got me through a very fast and very intense labor.

The midwife's experienced and skilled assistant, Cheryl, arrived before the midwife, and I was feeling very . . . mammalian. I was hypersensitive; I didn't want to be touched, and I didn't even want to be spoken to. I was operating from the primal brain for sure. I told her I was feeling funny, but my water had not broken. When Cheryl convinced me to let her check how many centimeters I was dilated, she said that the "funny feeling" was that it was time to push! I was shocked. I figured that I could not be very far along since I was handling things with a lot of focus and joy amid all the intensity. How could I have done this on my own? I wondered. My doula was at another birth, which we assumed would be over in plenty of time for her to come to mine. She sent her associate to our house. She walked in the door in time to introduce herself and then help me to the futon mattress on the floor to hold my hand as I pushed. After the first big push, my baby came out and the bag of water broke over his head and all over Cheryl. (This is referred to as a baby being born in the caul and it is quite unusual and special.) Cheryl then said with ample firmness in her voice, "Wait, wait—we've got a cord here!" My heart skipped a few beats, but I waited patiently as the midwife's assistant unwound the cord from about the baby's neck and torso with a few swift, graceful movements. My older son, almost three years old, watched all of this from his high chair. It was miraculous, fantastic, and ecstatic.

In Conclusion

What my births taught me is that I believe in my body's ability to birth. I trust that I know how to labor and my baby knows when to come out. Babies who are induced to come out, whether naturally or synthetically, are simply *not* ready. Every birth is different, and natural variability in all realms ought to be respected and not used to cause a mother anxiety or distress; accusing her body of not knowing what to do, or of not keeping to the timetable a hospital has established, is very dangerous indeed. The greatest impediment I found in my first labor was being told I couldn't do it, being told that I needed medical science to help me, and that fears, not faith, ought to govern my decisions.

Whatever you decide is right for you, try to keep an open mind and understand why people are so passionate about natural birth, even if you are not. Try not to view the need for education and support for this process as a sign that natural birth is *not* natural or that it is out of reach; rather, birthing without being raised in a culture that supports natural birth is what is incredibly hard, and there is work to be done to reclaim our intuitive knowledge, trust, and confidence about birth and labor. There are reasons why women choose natural birth, and it's not to be a martyr or be able to brag about it. Natural birth is an amazing and transformative experience that stays with you and your baby forever, and just think: you already know exactly how to do it perfectly.

4

Baby Needs Milk:
Why We Breastfeed

Within minutes of birth, a newborn displays a desire and a remarkable ability to nurse. There are incredible videos documenting newborns minutes old literally squirming to their mothers in order to latch on to the breast and nurse. As female mammals, we possess mammary glands that produce milk and milk ducts and nipples that allow for the secretion of milk for years upon years to nourish and nurture our young through their dependent stage of development. It is natural, it is beautiful and, tragically, it has been undermined both medically and socially since the beginning of the past century. There have been successful movements to reclaim breastfeeding, most notably started by La Leche League in 1958 and by the work of women activists in the 1970s, who also brought natural labor back to the forefront of our minds.

Fortunately for babies and their mothers, since the 1970s, breast-feeding has been supported and encouraged again to some extent, and the American Academy of Pediatrics (AAP), the World Health Organization, UNICEF, and most reputable medical authorities agree that breast is indeed best. However, there are still aggressive and misleading efforts to supply women with formula and to undermine breastfeeding (typically to increase corporations' profits). There are also individual cases of injustice done to women feeding their children in public places (I myself would be hard-pressed to find a mall or restaurant in the state of California whose customers and staff have not seen my breasts!), and there remain frightening misunderstandings about breastfeeding that are often passed on by women who mean well but are simply uneducated about the mechanics and benefits of breastfeeding.

Why Breastfeed?

I decided to become a certified lactation educator counselor (CLEC) after my second son was born, because I believe in the benefits of breastfeeding and I want to educate others about why and how to successfully breastfeed. As someone who struggled to nurse both of my sons, I wanted to help women who were also struggling. Why? Well, breastfeeding is enjoyable, it's ecologically wise, and it's incredibly convenient. It decreases the incidence of childhood illnesses and infections, benefits the overall health of the nursing mother, thus lowering health care costs, and in the words of what is widely regarded as the breastfeeding bible, *The Womanly Art of Breastfeeding* (8th edition), "There is almost nothing you can do for your child in his whole life that will affect him both emotionally and physically as profoundly as breastfeeding."

Breastfeeding takes getting used to, not only because it involves fluid leaving your body (sometimes at angles not predicted by New-tonian physics) but also because it is more than just a way to feed your baby. It is a lifestyle and a philosophy, and I believe that under-standing it as such will allow you to make the most educated decision about breastfeeding. Here are four reasons why breastfeeding should be the encouraged method of nourishment for humans:

1. Breastmilk is the best food for a human baby.

It is normal to feed your baby the milk that you, as a mammal, are designed to secrete from your body. Breastmilk is the most complete food there is, and it is nature's best protection against infection, respiratory problems, and intestinal challenges. The colostrum you produce from your breasts in the first days of your baby's life is made to move the meconium out of his body, seal his intestines, and establish the best flora in his guts for successful feeding and diges-tion. Artificial baby milk (cleverly referred to by manufacturers as "formula," as if babies were race cars needing to be supercharged!) cannot do any of those things the same way, because it is an artificial substitute for what nature created to do best.

2. Breastfeeding is good for mama.

Breastfeeding is a relationship between you and your baby, and you benefit from it, too. Breastfeeding may not make you lose weight overnight, and until you stop nursing, your body may hold on to a few extra pounds (we call it "milk fuel"), but you burn more than 300 calories a day simply sitting on your tush on the couch because your body is working to make milk, even when you are just watch-ing TV. Breastfeeding is associated with lower rates of several can-cers, including breast and ovarian. Why? Because we are naturally designed to nurse, and the hormones we have in our bodies when we nurse establish a special preferred and protected environment. Breastfeeding also lowers blood pressure and decreases your chances of osteoporosis and resulting bone fractures.

3. Breastfeeding builds an attachment unmatched by anything else.

Mammals were made to be nursed. The closeness, the touching, the cuddling, the attention and the care needed to make it all happen—these things make nursing the most reliable method to bond with your baby, successfully setting her up for a lifetime of emotional and psychological health and security. I am not saying that babies who are not breastfed are not held close, touched, cuddled, or attended to. We all know that women who bottle-feed (including those who cannot successfully nurse their babies but choose to bottle-feed with breastmilk) can bond with their babies, and they do. I am simply stating that the way nature designed us to keep our babies alive—by breastfeeding them—is not by accident. It's not just a convenience; it's a method of stimulating complicated hormones that connect us and keep us invested in each other. These hormones help us battle baby blues, they remind us to keep watch over our babies and foster positive and loving interactions between mothers and babies. It is the most natural, reliable way to ensure this bond, and it should be the goal of our world to see that every mother has all the education, resources, and support she needs to tip the scales toward bonding the way we were made to bond. The simplest way to state it is this: Breastfeeding does matter.

4. Breastfeeding is easy, even when it's hard.

Despite the challenges some women face, breastmilk is always available, it's always the right temperature, it's always the perfect flavor, you don't have to mix it or shake it (unless you really want to!), and if you need more, just plug the baby in, and—like magic—there is more! Breastmilk is free to make; just feed the mama routinely, give her plenty of water, and some well-deserved rest! Breastfeeding comforts children, but with closeness, warmth, and connection. Being a child's only source of nourishment for a little while may sound exhausting, but it made my parenting journey quite simple. A baby's fear, anxiety, overstimulation, lone-liness, and pain are all treated with nursing anytime, anywhere; and that's not unnatural; it's natural as can be. All children wean eventually, and there is no research that shows that breastfeeding on demand makes for spoiled or clingy children any more than not breastfeeding this way does.

Now that you can see the significance and importance of feeding your baby the normal, nature-designed perfect food, I want to share with you six startling things and six amazing things I have learned from nursing my two children for a total of five years (and count-ing). These dozen things, for me, comprise the twelve things I would tell anyone who is pregnant to consider and understand fully about breastfeeding.

Six Startling Things I Learned About Breastfeeding

1. Not everyone was made to nurse easily at first.

This one pissed me off. Some of us get off to a rocky start breastfeed-ing, and the first six weeks in particular can be, frankly, very chal-lenging and very discouraging. Our one job as a mammal mama is to keep the baby alive with our milk, and if we feel that we are not excelling at that one job, it sucks big-time (no pun intended).

Some women latch their newborns on right away, get a great photo of baby nursing contentedly while their supportive husband looks on adoringly, and never have any problems. I am superhappy for these women. (I am also super-resentful of them, but I am work-ing on that.)

Here is an almost complete list of issues I had with *both* of my boys several times *each:*

- soreness that made me cry out in pain as if I were being wounded in the gut (my husband's description) when baby latched on

- a need for over-the-counter medication to alleviate the early discomfort of nursing
- plugged ducts
- nursing blisters (think giant whitehead on your nipple—ouch!)
- mastitis (a treatable breast infection)
- cracked and broken skin on the nipples
- thrush (a treatable yeast infection on the nipple and/or inside of the breast)
- babies with a recessed chin (which can make latching on difficult at first)
- babies with too small a mouth relative to the nipple (ditto)
- and my personal favorite: "atypical" nipples. Hopefully my dad and my male friends will be so weirded out by this phrase that they will blot it out of their minds forever. For the rest of you, just know that, as any lactation consultant will tell you, there is hardly a nipple that cannot be nursed on. If you have inverted, pseudoinverted, or short-shanked/flat nipples, you can nurse. I promise. Trust me. Can we just leave it at that?

The first six weeks are very hard for some of us, but now that I have told you that, I have saved you some of the shock that I speak to so many women about. When I started nursing and was having difficulty, I was uncertain about whether I was doing it "right," so immediately—meaning in the first days of difficulty—I sought help from La Leche League (LLL). It was there that I found moms who had experienced these things and had gotten through them! Several amazing (and very flexible, supportive, and nonjudgmental) La Leche League leaders took my calls at all hours, when I was in various states of hysteria, fear, uncertainty, or all of the above. These are the women who walked me through my first months of nursing the way female primates have done for one another for millions of years.

I have stayed in touch with my La Leche League leaders, and when we see them in our neighborhood, at the park, or in the market,

I tell my sons with a tear in my eye: "Those are the women who helped you have milky." Having this support system made me feel less alone, less abnormal, and more able to find the help I needed to get through those weeks, after which *anything* was easier!

2. The baby is okay before your milk comes in.

Within two to five days after birth, the colostrum that your body has been producing since you were pregnant changes into true breast-milk. Our bodies evolved this way for a reason, and there is nothing wrong with a healthy baby who is free of complications nursing on just colostrum until your milk comes in. Yes, your baby is eager to suck, and yes, your baby may cry a little, but crying could be normal, and tiny tummies only need colostrum in those early days.

A lot of women are pressured to give their babies formula because their husbands (or their doctors or their mothers-in-law or someone else) could not stand the sound of a crying baby. Get over it, people. It's a newborn. It cries; that's part of the job description. Giving in to pressure from people who recommend that you give formula because your "milk is not coming in fast enough" is risking nipple confusion, when the baby learns to prefer a bottle and refuses the breast. More significantly, formula is not necessary before your milk comes in. All mammals wait until their milk comes in and you can, too. Listen to your instincts and your baby, and know that your baby will not be left behind by evolution.

It should be noted that the most successful breastfeeding out-comes result from unmedicated natural births. Drugs can both in-hibit milk coming in as well as make the baby a less efficient nurser due to drugs in her bloodstream. Women who give birth by cesarean section (which are, by definition, medicated births) may have lower success rates for these reasons as well as the fact that the stress of surgery and recovery can inhibit milk coming in. Women who have medicated births, C-sections, excessive stress, poor diets, and very active social calendars within days of giving birth can, of course, nurse successfully—there are many different paths to successful breastfeeding. But keep in mind that if we want to do our best to ensure a healthy breastfeeding relationship, it behooves us to do our absolute best to minimize factors that might challenge this relationship at its inception.

As a general guideline, tons of rest, a well-rounded diet, sufficient water consumption, and minimal stress and activity will all increase the probability of milk coming in quickly and staying at the right level for your baby.

A note on "having enough milk": It is incredibly rare for a woman to not make enough milk, although women are told that they don't have enough milk all the time, typically by people who know very little about breastfeeding. There are many factors that go into having and maintaining a good milk supply, which takes at least six weeks to stabilize. In those three months, nursing on demand with no supplements, pacifiers, or bottles is critical to stack the chips on your side. Co-sleeping and keeping baby close (two other facets of attachment parenting that we'll talk about later) facilitate frequent stimulation of the breasts and the hormones by nursing, for strong milk production and supply.

I know it is tempting to hand the baby over to someone for a few feedings here and there without waking up to pump so that you can get some sleep. And ultimately, you have to make the choice that is right for you. But something that doctors and caregivers don't always communicate clearly to new moms is that skipping feedings in the early weeks and months increasingly tells your body it does not need to make milk, and this can lead to a drop in milk supply. If you're told that you are not making enough milk, and breastfeeding is important to you, get help right away to keep it going—it's worth it.

3. It is normal for a newborn baby to nurse a LOT for the first weeks.
When my husband was born in 1975, his mother was sent home from the hospital with specific instructions to feed him only every four hours. She was baffled by nightfall, though, because he was hungry

every two! She did not have the support to know that it was okay to nurse him on demand, and she ended up feeling frustrated and confused about what was best for her baby.

The good news today: we now encourage women to nurse on demand, meaning: *whenever the baby wants to.* In the early weeks, this can mean pretty much feeling plugged in to the baby all day and all night, if not with your nipple in their mouth, then at least with them near your breast and in your arms. In the early weeks, both of my newborns would often nurse more than a half hour on each breast and fall asleep there after a full nursing, only to wake up thirty minutes later and do it all again. I was exhausted and literally pinned down to the couch for the better part of those early weeks. But it is so important to know that this is not abnormal and it is totally fine to do this. If you are experiencing soreness and discomfort, seek the advice of a lactation professional to see if other ways of having the baby close without your nipple getting a lot of "use" would be better for your breasts and nipples. Every baby is different, and so is every breast!

As mentioned above, a woman's milk supply does not fully stabilize until at least six weeks postpartum, so all the nursing done in those early weeks is laying the foundation for a strong milk supply and a great nursing relationship. In addition, when babies have growth spurts, their increased nursing is signaling your body to make more milk, not that you don't have enough or that you can't make enough milk. It's that the baby's job is to demand that you make an adequate supply for their changing needs and growth. It's your job to meet the demand.

4. Problems with nursing don't mean you have to stop.

With both of my boys, I was tempted to give up nursing many times in the first months. I had so many problems, and there was a period of weeks when every time the baby rooted or indicated it was time to nurse, I cringed and was close to tears. This was *not* how I imagined it would be.

However, I have been repaid a thousandfold for every struggle I had nursing. No one could have made me believe it then, but nursing my boys has been the most incredible, life-affirming, and healthy thing I have done for them and for myself. As I said before, if you have problems, this doesn't mean you were not made to nurse. Problems may simply mean that your genes are sneaking in under the wire or that you need a little guidance. Throughout primate history, females who were not naturally gifted at nursing, for whatever reason, did not have to nurse and could get someone else to nurse their babies. In this way, their genes got passed on through their children who might not have survived had they not had someone else to provide their babies milk. So I like to say that my genes may be weak in this area, but my resolve is strong, and my support network is broad and fierce, and that is how I gave my children—and myself—this precious gift.

5. Not every husband digs nursing talk.

This bears little explanation. Just as some guys want to watch the baby crowning and really truly do think you look beautiful as you push your watermelon-sized baby out into the world, some guys don't much enjoy that. Mine didn't.

And he also did not, does not, and will never, ever, dig nursing or breast talk. He was supportive and stoic as I cried and doubted myself and my breasts with both of our boys, but he simply did not want the details of what the right nipple looked like today versus the left, how much it hurt, and in what way and how I feared my breasts would never be the same again. Frankly, I think he had some of the same concerns about how my breasts would look in the future— that's probably why he was not very interested in this line of talk. But instead of trying to get him to enjoy discussing which cream I should apply to which nipple first and with which cotton swab, I got my nursing support elsewhere, from people who lived and breathed—and sometimes even got paid to live and breathe—breasts and breastfeeding. Which leads me to my final point . . .

6. Support is critical.

If I did not have support, education, and resources, I could not have nursed my boys. I am not exaggerating to make a point; it's simply the truth. There are women who give their time and lives to help other women breastfeed because they believe strongly that it is a birthright for a child and a blessing for a mother to nurse. Breast-feeding classes are offered to pregnant women at hospitals as well as breastfeeding and maternity stores. And the amazing organization La Leche League offers meetings that are free and open to pregnant and nursing moms. I recommend learning as much as you can about breastfeeding *before* you are faced with a hungry little one nuzzling at your chest. You don't need to have a nursing baby yet to benefit from hearing about women who nurse. It gets you familiar with ter-minology and lets you hear about the nursing lifestyle: the decisions, choices, and benefits, as well as the challenges.

Thousands of hospitals have lactation consultants on staff, but it is not fair for women to be supposedly encouraged to breastfeed without knowledge of what to do if things go wrong once they get home from the hospital. When I was pregnant with our first son, we chose a pediatrician who is not only a certified lactation consultant but employs a lactation nurse on his staff. Within days of our son's birth, I was in desperate need of help, and the nurse came to our house to coach and instruct me. With our second son, another lacta-tion nurse visited me to do it all over again. Knowing who to call and how to ask for help within hours of a problem can sometimes be critical to your nursing relationship, since one seemingly minor nurs-ing issue can quickly snowball into bigger problems. It should be a priority in our culture to provide women with ample and inexpensive lactation support, since nursing has the potential to decrease medical costs and taxpayer funds for babies and their mothers, as well as providing every child who is nursed the opportunity to bond and be nourished the way nature intended it.

Six Amazing Things I Learned About Breastfeeding

1. People on planes love you and your nursling.

I am one of those people who really dreads kids on my airplane flights—other people's kids, I mean. When I see them with their little backpacks, looking so perky and excited to board, I can't help but picture hours of screaming for candy or another DVD, violent tantrums . . . and exhausted and overwhelmed parents who can't decide if they should give in or risk further escalation of the situation by not giving in.

When I first flew with our first baby, I was so anxious that I would be "that parent." I read up on flying with a newborn and tried really hard to time his nursing before boarding so that he would be sufficiently motivated and hungry to nurse on takeoff (to protect tiny ears from painful pressurizing). What I learned on that first flight more than six years ago has been true on every single flight I have taken in the years since: breastfed babies who are nursed on demand are usually really pleasant on planes.

Breastmilk contains chemicals that induce sleep, and the only thing better than a quiet awake baby on a plane is a sleeping one, if you ask me. As an added plus, the roar of the plane provides a sort of white noise that allowed my boys to nap longer on planes than they ever did in real life, and since nursing is a little nursling's favorite thing to do, they never minded being plugged in for longer than they might be at home. I sometimes wished I could hop on a plane at naptime to get them to sleep more than their favored forty-minute naptime stretches of sleep! Plus, nursing when you travel just makes life easier. Period. On outings or unexpected delays in our travels all over the United States and through the Middle East, I have never worried about my nursing child, because breastmilk is always available, always the right temperature, and always completely nutritious and satisfying.

Add to the above the fact that nursing babies who are swallowing and gulping on takeoff and landing are doing the equivalent of gum chewing to help open up their ears, and you have the makings of a beautiful life jet-setting with your nursing baby. And if you happen to make babies who have a strong desire to walk or run about once they are mobile, flying may turn out to be hellish for you. So, my advice to people with young babies is this: travel as much as you can before your baby is mobile. It will never be easier than it is right now, especially with a happily nursing baby in tow.

2. Breastmilk changes over time.

Breastmilk is the most complete and nutritious food for human babies. According to the AAP, babies should nurse *exclusively* for at least six months with no solids or formula or water given at all. After six months, you can start solids, but there are those among us who do not give any solids until a year of age, for a variety of reasons including dietary, allergy-related, and philosophical.

Aside from breastmilk being an amazing and perfect food, it truly has properties that can be described only as magical. Among the many miraculous things breastmilk can do—which no formula has ever been created to reproduce—is that it actually changes its fat content over time according to the needs and development of your baby. When a baby is born, the milk is high in fat, which is necessary to help the brain develop while insulating the body. The highest-fat milk is called hindmilk, and it is delivered only to the baby in the second half of a nursing session, as if to ensure that babies nurse long enough at each opportunity. The baby is thus rewarded with the highest-fat milk only after a good nursing session. A word of warning to moms with babies who like to frequently start to nurse but quickly fall asleep: eating only the soup course at a meal over and over never lets you get to the heartier main course. If you have a baby who likes to fall asleep at the breast, wake her up and get past the soup course so that she can get the important higher-fat main course in her tummy!

As babies get older, the way they nurse changes. They nurse more efficiently, it takes less time for their suck to release milk (one sign of an experienced nurser), and nursing sessions get shorter overall (which is also due to increased activity by the baby, who wants to look around and play as soon as he can). The magical part is that breastmilk will adjust to ensure that your older nurser is still getting enough calories, fat, protein, and vitamins by changing the percentages of these elements in your milk. The one thing that doesn't change, though, is the level of antibodies in your breastmilk. So a newborn, a one-year-old, and a three-year-old all get the benefit of your antibodies; your body knows how much to concentrate those sickness- and disease-fighting superpowers depending on how frequently your baby nurses! Incredible!

No formula can do any of this, and that is one of the reasons traditional size charts used by pediatrician's offices to measure your child's growth often misjudge the health of a breastfed baby: some women make higher-fat milk than others, but babies nursed on demand cannot be obese, never overnurse, and have a higher chance for healthy body weight as they become children, teenagers, and adults.

My boys were so plump that there were a few pediatrician's visits in the first year when my older son was above the ninety-ninth percentile. I received a lot of unwanted and cruel comments about my sons' bodies both from people on the street and in my family: "He's so fat!" "You must be overfeeding him!" "Wow! He looks like he's a good eater; what on earth are you feeding him?" But my favorite was a comment someone posted on a website that featured a paparazzi photo of me in an airport in New York with Fred, who was twenty-eight pounds at twelve months: "That's not cute. He looks really unhealthy; he is way too big."

It should be noted that there are also breastfed babies who are petite and healthy as well; these babies are often accused by breast-feeding skeptics of being underweight and failing to thrive even when they hit all of their developmental milestones, are not fussy, and act well-nourished and content. Pediatricians and laypersons alike often recommend to these confused mothers that they fatten up their babies with high-calorie dairy products and, of course, supplement with cow's milk formula, even when the mothers have an innate sense that their babies are fine and are simply petite. Remember that you are the best judge of how your baby is behaving and growing, not a chart or a random person on the street or on the Internet.

Both of my boys are now of average weight and height, and I look back at their first years as a pleasure: nursing plump, rosy-cheeked, happy boys who were as tall as they were heavy, and who seemed to soak up every ounce of magic that I poured into them by breastfeeding.

3. Breastmilk is nature's miracle medicine.

Besides its nutritive properties and its ability to bond an infant to its mother with intensity and unabashed intimacy, did you know that breastmilk has many other uses? There are several ways we used breastmilk for our boys besides just as food.

- Applied to cracked or tender nipples: it's the one nipple cream you *know* does not need to be wiped off before nursing again!
- Squirted in tiny noses on airplanes or anywhere germs seek to land and make homes in sensitive nasal passages; the milk provides a coating of the nasal membrane and the tickle factor encourages sneezing out of said germs.
- Dripped into eyes with plugged ducts, redness, or signs of infection (check with your pediatrician first to rule out a more serious problem).

- Used on diaper rash; does not make the tush smelly or sticky; it simply absorbs and works incredibly.
- Used on baby acne, heat rash, and other skin bumps.
- Did you know that superfleshy, roly-poly babies, even if bathed regularly, can accumulate a very nasty stinky substance in the folds of their armpits, necks (and multiple chins), and groins? Fred's armpits would get so irritated from the aforementioned stinky stuff that his skin would start to crack. Guess what? Breastmilk makes it go away and heals the skin at the same time! Amazing.
- Dropped into ears during the common cold to prevent the development of ear infection.
- Rubbed on ingrown toenails (this one shocked me!). I waited patiently for weeks with no luck for Fred's tiny ingrown toenail to grow out and for the redness and swelling to go away. Then I tried breastmilk: it was healed in a day.
- Dabbed on cuts and scrapes: it is a natural antibiotic! Once he weaned, my older son started to balk when I tried to use breastmilk on his boo-boos, so I would put a drop of it onto his Band-Aids unbeknownst to him and then bring in the Band-Aid . . . does this make me a bad mom? I hope not.

See the Resources section at the end of the book for the recommended method of easy and safe hand-expression that makes all of the following possible and convenient. Alternatively, you can use pumped breastmilk in the same ways.

4. Breastmilk comforts when words can't.

The idea that nursing is not just for nutrition makes a lot of people uncomfortable, and I can understand that. Especially in our modern culture, the closeness and intimacy of nursing, especially once a child is "old enough to ask for it," is hard for some people to understand. In addition, I was not the kind of mom who wanted nursing to be how I made my kids feel better if they fell down and got hurt, or if they were sad. It just wasn't something my husband and I wanted to have as our first parenting tool. For the most part, when my boys got hurt as babies, I nursed immediately, and as they got older, I made the decision not to use breastfeeding as a first resort when a child needed soothing. This worked very well most of the time.

However, there have been those moments when nothing would do but the milky. The boob. Nonnies. Nummies. Nachos. Whatever you call it, it really is phenomenally soothing when nothing else is working and the need is there. I nursed both of my boys when they took hard falls or bumps, and nursing calmed everyone down when all I could see was red—the red of blood seeping through tiny teeth! Nursing connects mama and child back to their first connection and their first intimacy, and sometimes all it takes is that connection to ground a little person who is hurting.

I will not go into how long this comfort ought to be available for a child, because that is a very personal and very complicated decision. As for me, I support natural child-led (sometimes mama-encouraged) weaning when the child shows readiness, with boundaries established as soon as they need to be for maximum mother and child comfort. I nursed my older son just over two years, and my little guy, at over three years, still nurses about five times in a twenty-four-hour period, including on demand at night or when he asks or needs to during the day. I do not pass judgment when I see four- and even five- or six-year-olds still nursing. I know it would not work for me to nurse a child that large and mature, but I also firmly believe that you know your child better than I do, and it behooves me to realize that one person's two-year-old is another person's six-month-old. It's amazing how many people think nothing of commenting directly to a mom when they think a kid is "too old" to breastfeed. For example, I was asked by plenty of people how long I intended to nurse—even when my boys were not yet old enough to sit up straight, much less walk, talk, or "ask for it."

(As a mother, you'll soon learn that some random strangers' nosiness knows no bounds.)

I am aware that nursing a plus-thirty-pound "baby" (as I did with my older son and still do with my younger) has a stigma, so I do my best to meet my child's needs while also maintaining a degree of comfort in the social situations I find myself in when the need to nurse strikes. I have found that showing others the respect to have their opinions softens their judgment of me, and they give me the room to demonstrate my opinion by sometimes lifting up my shirt and nursing discreetly.

This seems an appropriate time to mention how very important it is to invest in a few simple nursing tops. The money I spent for the nursing clothes I bought were so worth it: to be able to nurse anywhere and at any time and to not be limited by having your belly or your breasts exposed cannot be overemphasized. Feeling protected (at whatever level of modesty you believe in) made me more confident that I could meet my child's needs when they arose. I favored nursing tanks and shirts that had two layers of fabric: one that lifted up and one that stayed against my belly (typically with some sort of opening to let baby find the breast). I bought a black nursing tank, a white one, too, and two or three sturdy long-sleeved cotton T-shirts that lasted me through both of my sons' first years. I also purchased an underwire-free, nice nursing bra (underwire can plug ducts and interfere with milk production) and a dressier nursing top, in black, that I wore with tailored skirts and a nice sweater, jacket, or scarf if I was invited to some event that required more than a T-shirt and a peasant skirt, which was sort of my uniform during my early nursing months.

5. Breastfeeding allows for the earliest lessons in discipline and cooperative behavior.

Babies are born needing guidance. They are—neurobiologically speaking—helpless, undeveloped, and dependent on us for their very survival. The early weeks and months of breastfeeding are the first lessons you teach your baby. You teach them how to get nourishment and what the boundaries are for that relationship: how to open wide so that they don't hurt your nipples, how repeated attempts at something difficult invariably gets easier (nursing can be hard for babies, too!), and how to signal cues reliably and faithfully.

As your baby gets older, breastfeeding allows you to teach your child in the closest possible way which behaviors are acceptable and unacceptable (i.e., pulling your hair, squeezing your nose, fondling the other breast while nursing), and eventually, you get to explore the concept of boundaries and needs as your child matures and weans. This is not to say that women who don't breastfeed do not get to teach their children boundaries or discipline; rather, those of us who do breastfeed get an interaction that forces us to teach the lessons right away. Without breastfeeding, you teach them through a myriad of other situations and interactions, but breastfeeding, for me, provided a wonderful and readily available delivery system for discipline and the establishment of healthy boundaries that have endured past weaning.

6. You will get over your fears.

I was never a particularly vain woman, and I don't consider myself one now. However, once I decided to breastfeed, the fear I had that my breasts would never be the same was real. I had fears that my husband would feel left out if I nursed, since he couldn't. I often felt "touched out," and I had a lot of fear that I would never want to be touched again because I was being touched *all the time* by my nurslings.

Well, guess what? My breasts are the breasts of a thirty-six-year-old mother of two. But I never looked like those women in magazines before I had kids anyway, so I don't really feel like I'm missing out now. (That's why there are magazines that cater to nursing moms: we *can* look like the women in *those* magazines!) I embrace my body (breasts and all) because this is the body that carried my children, birthed them, and nourished them. My husband connects with our children in hundreds of ways, and he does not feel at all pushed out of their lives simply because he was born with a Y chromosome. Women are made to breastfeed, and he understands and respects that. We love our kids, and everything about our parenting is factored into our relationship with them. The fears I had of being touched out did not last forever, and it all changes and shifts in a marriage all the time anyway. This is our life now, and when we look at our boys, we remember that they are what it's all for.

Some women truly cannot nurse, and many feel a deep sense of loss about this. Some women do not want to nurse, and they feel a deep sense of pride in their decision. I can't say what is right for every woman, but I can say that with the proper resources, support, and education, I would hope that many more women would embrace what their bodies were made to do, even if only for a day, a week, a month, a year . . . One day is better than no days nursing, one week is better than six days, and any time a child is at the breast, it's good for all involved.

5

Baby Needs to Be Held: How Will You Ever Get Anything Done Ever Again?

Many people assume that I must have "easy" kids. As babies, both of my boys were very quiet and mellow, and they were almost always smiling and happy. They never had colic (in fact, they rarely cried longer than a few minutes), they sat nicely in high chairs, and they never had tantrum problems. People would often say how easy I had it as they regaled me with stories of obstinance, violent outbursts, and colic (when what they described did not even meet the clinical criteria for colic).

I would nod sympathetically, but I assure you that my boys are not easy and they never were. On the contrary, they were what many refer to as "high needs" babies: they had a lot of wants and requirements both day and night (which they always made very clear to us!), and my husband and I chose to meet those needs to the best of our ability. What that looked like in the first weeks and months of their lives, however, is that they needed to be held a lot. And I mean *a lot*.

Babies Want to Be Held

Before I had my first son, I had a somewhat realistic—if theoretical—picture of how hard it would be having a baby. Like many eager expectant moms, I did a lot of reading about healing from birth, postpartum adjusting, breastfeeding, and newborn behavior and care. I imagined sleepless nights (having no clue what "totally, completely, and utterly exhausted" actually meant), sore nipples (having no clue what painful, tender, and sore would really feel like), and feeling overwhelmed (having no clue what true, pushed-to-the-limit, maxed-out parenthood would truly look like).

What I was not prepared for was one small but critically important reality of having a new baby: they really like to be held.

And I'm not just talking about "Oh, it's so nice to hold this baby! Boy, does this baby love holding! This baby smells yummy! It's so much fun to hold a little body that is so delicate and tiny!" No. I mean that some babies will not—let me repeat that—will *not* be happy unless they are being held. And it's not always cute or fun or adorable when they make that clear to you.

When my first son was born, I was frankly shocked by his intense and unrelenting desire to be held. I was also very perturbed: did he not understand that I had things to do? People to see? Chores to manage? Sleep to catch up on? In true scientist fashion, I became rather methodical about trying to figure out precisely why he wanted to be held so much and how I could stop this alarming desire of his.

I set out to find a situation where he would be content to *not* be held. Perhaps he would like to be put down when he was full of milk.

No? Okay, perhaps he wants to be put down while already asleep. That just wakes him up? Okay. Maybe he would let me put him down if he fell asleep *without* my breast in his mouth? No? Maybe I could put him down *with* my breast in his mouth and then sneak it out and walk away? Still no? Okay. So . . . that's: no, no, no, and no. He really just wanted to be held. Nursed and rocked and held. And sometimes just to mix it up a little, he'd spit up. And then he wanted to be held some more.

Now, I know what you're thinking. You are thinking that I could simply not tolerate a baby fussing, and if I would have just let him be for a minute, an hour, or a short stretch, then he would have decided he was fine (and he'd have stopped fussing and he would graduate at the top of his medical school class). You think I spoiled my babies and am to blame for their strong need to be held.

In my case, that's not what was going on. Some babies make it very clear that they need to be held, and I intuitively concluded that my babies absolutely had that need. And so I held them. A lot. Maybe sort of . . . all the time at first. And kind of sort of all the time for the first few weeks. And now that I think about it, pretty much most of the day and night for a good couple of months. That's a lot of holding.

Our Solution Is Babywearing

In the early weeks after their birth, my babies would nurse and fall asleep on me, and I would stay that way for hours on end on our couch: resting, checking email, working on my thesis from my computer, and catching up on phone calls. The laundry did not get done very efficiently in those early weeks. The refrigerator was not stocked full of scrumptious, delightful, and healthy home-cooked meals. I did not have lunch with friends or go out for drinks, much less get any fresh air or exercise. And sometimes I was just plain tired of holding my baby. I wanted to feel unencumbered, even if it was just so that I could go to the bathroom or walk to the mailbox without holding a baby. This holding pattern (as it were) could not go on forever. Life was knocking at my door and I had to figure out a way to answer it while still meeting the needs of my boys.

As it is for many parents who resonate with this particular aspect of attachment parenting, the solution that works for us is babywearing. "Babywearing" is the general term for having your baby close to your body in a baby carrier that allows your hands to be free. Babywearing was the answer to many of the challenges I faced with a high-needs baby. It is one of the most important things you can do to ensure that your baby has a smooth transition from the safety and cuddly warmth of your womb to the outside world, which is chock-full of sensory overload and way too much space in which tiny limbs—and minds—tend to flail about with no sense of containment. Babywearing regulates a baby, protects him from overstimulation, and promotes a content, calm, and securely attached baby-parent relationship. It is no wonder that cultures that carry their babies on their bodies rarely report colic!

Once my immediate postpartum period ended, I started experimenting with different carriers until I found the ones that worked best for us and our lifestyle. Here are examples of the most commonly used carriers, all of which are designed to be used (with a little instruction and practice) with baby facing in, out, or on your back:

- **Over-the-shoulder:** This is a sling made from a simple piece of fabric that you slip over your head. Nursing is very comfortable and discreet in this kind of sling. Some brands require no adjustments but are suited to your body size (known as pouch slings), whereas the ring-sling variety of over-the-shoulder slings uses a simple metal ring that anchors the fabric at your shoulder and is adjustable so that it can be used by people of varying heights easily, such as a mama and a dada. If I had to pick one sling to own, it would be a ring sling for sure, and my husband agrees!

- **Structured carrier:** This kind of carrier uses ties or clips to secure the straps. We used this kind of sling for non-nursing-heavy outings, since I found it challenging to nurse in a structured pack. I still carried our three-year-old (most packs can handle up to thirty-five or forty pounds) on my back in the same structured pack he rode around in on my tummy as a newborn. I don't find a structured carrier convenient to use when, for example, running errands and needing to have baby in and out of your arms a lot, but it's great to strap on a carrier like this for longer outings such as hikes or trips to crowded places where you want baby to see things from a safe vantage point, as opposed to from a stroller or on foot.

- **Wrap:** This is a very long, flexible, cozy piece of fabric with no clasps that can be tied in numerous ways. These take a little practice, but many people—once the preferred positions are mastered—rely on wraps specifically for their versatility. I liked a wrap for walking with my newborns, especially when we were just learning to nurse in the sling, as the fabric allowed for a lot of adjustments when shifting positions. This kind of carrier is a great one for babies to face out from without the unnatural positioning that most commercial outward-facing carriers use (see Tip #1 on page 84).

Within weeks of wearing my baby, my life was transformed. I was off the couch, taking walks around the neighborhood, cooking meals at the stove, straightening up around the house (even vacuuming!), and running simple errands without ever upsetting the baby or lifting a pricey and bulky car seat or stroller. I did not have to leave events or parties when it was time for baby to sleep, since babywearing meant that my boys could nurse and nap on me anywhere we were. I have given our boys naps while wearing them more often than I haven't: in the supermarket, at synagogue, in conferences, in meetings, and even while strolling on the Las Vegas Strip.

Every carrier has a different weight limit, but most can carry up to thirty-five or forty pounds, and I was able to wear my almost thirty-five-pound toddler well into my second pregnancy, even while hiking in Hawai'i. Babywearing has opened up my life and allowed me to be an active person again, not someone pinned to the couch all of the time. Babywearing has given me my sanity back, because even a mother who loves holding her baby eventually needs to feel a little bit "normal" again.

For most of human history, babies have been worn for much of the first years of their lives. Cultures all over the world have had special ways to wear babies so that they were protected, cuddled, easily nursed, and secure. Babies in the arctic were held in fur-lined carriers worn under clothing, Native American babies were swaddled in a papoose, and babies in Papua New Guinea were carried in nets draped over one's head. Every culture has found ways to carry their babies that allow the parents freedom and provide the babies comfort and closeness. Cultures that carry their babies on their bodies often report that babies gain weight more reliably than babies who are not held close, due largely to the fact that frequent nursing and stimulation of milk-making hormones are facilitated by close contact with the milk source. Carried babies also tend to take shorter naps, thus maximizing nursing time. Babies like to watch the world go by from the vantage point of your arms. They learn how it feels when you lift groceries, what your voice sounds like as you talk to the mailman, and how you hold yourself when you meet someone new. These are all valuable lessons, and babies learn a tremendous amount from being a part of your day on your body, rather than simply an observer from afar.

Babywearing is not just for mothers, either. My husband and I shared a simple ring sling. Our boys were accustomed to always nursing to sleep, and there was no way for my husband to replicate that. I never dreamed that he would ever be able to put our boys down for a nap, but babywearing changed that: he was able to lull our boys to sleep because they simply loved to sleep in a sling.

We have all seen new parents lugging around cumbersome (if stylish) car-seat carriers. If you ask them about it, they often force a smile and proclaim through gritted teeth, "Now I don't have to wake the baby to get him in and out of the car!" What they don't tell you about, though, is how heavy a baby gets to be in a car-seat carrier, how you can very easily get a pinched nerve or other muscle or joint pain in the arm and shoulder you use to schlep the car-seat carrier around, and how awkward and sometimes impossible it can be to maneuver around most restaurants or stores with one of those devices.

It is true that if your baby is sleeping in the car, it can be a drag to wake him. But I guarantee you that you will figure out what works for you and your family, and you can indeed function without relying on a car-seat carrier or stroller all the time. We had kids who never stayed asleep if we attempted to move them from where they fell asleep. If we had plans to meet someone for lunch and the baby fell asleep in the car on the way, one of us simply waited until he woke up, or we shifted our plans. We could not justify using a car-seat carrier for the handful of times that happened. And we all turned out okay, I promise!

I sometimes joke that there seems to be an underlying message in our culture that screams: "Don't touch the baby! Whatever you do, *don't touch the baby*!" You can transport your baby from car-seat carrier to car to stroller and back again, and I would imagine you can go for hours without any real physical contact with your child. I've seen mothers go through entire meals in restaurants without much more than a glance at their baby in a car-seat carrier, except to position a pacifier or bottle in their mouths.

Babies need contact with us and with our bodies. We smell familiar, we sound good, and we feel right. They want to be held close *to* us, not simply *next to* us.

Six Tips for Easier Babywearing

For many parents who have tried it (myself included), wearing a baby can be a hugely important part of one's parenting philosophy. In fact, to me it's really a part of my lifestyle. What do I mean by that? Well, babywearing is much more than just purchasing a cute outfit-matching swatch of fabric. Those of us who are passionate about babywearing have done our research, and we can tell you not just the stats of why it's better, but how to actually put it into practice. Read on for some hard-won wisdom on how to do it gracefully, and why wearing your baby is one of the most freeing things a new parent can do.

1. Beware the outward-facing, structured (tremendously popular) carrier.

One of the most popular carriers that I see on city streets positions your baby facing out, with the baby's back to your tummy. Moms and dads alike love these kinds of carriers because they need no tying, minor adjusting, and these carriers are advertised prominently. I know you are going to call me a wet blanket for saying anything bad about them . . . but I can't help myself: *babies should face you tummy to tummy, rather than with their back to your tummy, for the better part of the first year.*

Babies don't need a lot of stimulation in the early months, and many babies find it upsetting to be faced with so much stimuli when facing out; heck, I'm a grown adult and *I* get overstimulated by a lot of what I see on any given day on the streets of Los Angeles! Many times I have seen fussy and cranky outward-facing babies who are clearly overstimulated by a loud and confusing environment, angry hands to their faces and tiny eyes closing in protest. The less recognized expressions of overstimulation are babies cowering or becoming overly docile and withdrawn; many people mistake a terrified baby for a "good" one, and it is worth learning some of these subtle differences! You carried your baby for almost ten months inside of you. For the first ten months of life outside of you, encourage your baby to see and smell and nuzzle and be held close to the face and body and voice and world that she knows best: yours!

2. Soft carriers are better than structured ones.

The second thing to be aware of about the popular structured outward-facing carriers is that they tend to force baby's body into unnatural positions: legs splayed out when they want to curl in for the first months, pressure on the crotch when the tush is a better source of padding and situating, arms flailing freely when they still need to be naturally held close to the body . . . There are ways to still give your baby the outward experience in a soft and more ergonomically favorable carrier when they are ready: don't be afraid to try one out; it's not rocket science, it's wearing your baby.

3. Different carriers are better for different situations.

As I mentioned in the descriptions of the different types of carriers, each carrier can serve a different purpose. We found that owning one sling and one structured carrier suited all of our needs; the former was used by both my husband and me for running errands, giving naps, and general everyday living. The latter we used for running through airports (especially when our city of destination had a friend who could loan us a stroller; who needs to schlep a stroller through airport security if you don't need to?), hiking, or activities like going to farmers' markets or crowded places where a lot of walking would be too strenuous for a little person and a stroller would not be a convenient option.

As you can see, choosing the carrier that is right for you helps babywearing become a lifestyle, not a trend or a product to be displayed. It becomes a relationship and a connection, a place to feel safe and to share the world from the same physical location in space: your body. When my older son reached the age of weaning and wasn't nursing to sleep anymore, he would often ask for "sling-sling." The motion of me walking him in the sling must have felt to him like he was my newborn again, and that lulled him to sleep when nursing couldn't anymore. There is a carrier for every purpose; find yours!

4. Babywearing is great for discreet nursing.

Babywearing facilitates successful nursing by allowing baby easy access to the smell of you, which reminds them to go ahead and latch on. However, sometimes (most times?) babies want to "latch on" when you are out trying to live your life, just merrily going about your business. This startled me in the early days of nursing, because it was my intention when I started out nursing in public to be discreet, and I couldn't figure out how I would ever get to be discreet if my little nurser wanted to uncover my breasts regardless of where I happened to be! Using a baby carrier allows for discreet nursing no matter where you are. I have nursed on nature walks, in supermarkets and post offices, in restaurants and at black-tie weddings, through airports and malls without anyone knowing; all people see is a happy baby tucked into a carrier.

5. Babywearing is a great way to include your partner.

There are many things I did with our babies that my husband couldn't. Examples include nursing (for obvious reasons), cleaning cradle cap with baby oil and a tiny comb (he dislikes oil on his hands), baby massage (ditto), and cutting finger- and toenails (he is a tad nervous that he will slip and our child will go through life saying, "Dada cut my finger off"). But the one thing that my husband—and any partner!—can do just as well (if not better) is to wear the baby. Babies love being held close to the source of the deep voice of a father, and they love the warmth that dads often give off, thanks to the testosterone-fueled chest hair prevalent among many men of our species. Dads are just as competent at holding babies as moms are, and because men are generally bigger and weigh more than women (I did top out at my husband's ideal weight in pregnancy #1, mind you), I have found that dads are great at carrying baby for an even longer time than we sometimes like to. My husband was a master at putting our older son to sleep in a sling, after which he could transition him to bed. When I would try to do this as a break from repeated nursings, our son could sense me next to him in a horizontal position . . . and you know what little nurslings most like to do when horizontal with their mamas: nurse! That defeated the purpose for me! Encouraging your partner to wear your baby allows them to feel empowered and appreciated for their special skills, which is not only important for baby but builds trust and cooperative love between a couple.

6. Even if you have a bad back, you can wear your baby.
With few exceptions, there is a carrier that can work for you. Breastfeeding stores usually have carriers that you can try on so that you can find the one that's right for you. I know it's tempting to simply buy the one that "everyone" is using, which comes in a nice box and looks so easy and convenient. But it's kind of like buying shoes: you can, in theory, buy shoes online that can be slipped on and come in one of two colors. They will do the trick and get you from point A to point B, but they may not be as comfortable or good for your feet, posture, and lifestyle as they could be. If you want to have shoes that feel like they were made for you, shoes that are comfortable but also functional (and stylish!), spend more time and effort to shop around. Now imagine that these shoes had the potential to give you freedom and a feeling of connectedness; an ease in living and functioning that you didn't think possible. If this were the case (and I believe it is), I would think you would want to take even more time and effort to find the baby carrier that is really right for you and your needs. *Mothering* magazine published an

award-winning article in 2007 that details everything you should consider when shopping for a baby carrier (see the Resources section) and I recommend it highly.

"But . . . My Baby Doesn't Want to Be Held!"

When a baby requests to be held, it triggers something very instinctual in us: the desire to meet the needs of our babies. This desire is ingrained in us as much as keeping them alive is ingrained in us. The need for holding and closeness is not a manipulation or evidence of a spoiled child. Rather, it is an expression of healthy dependence and a desire for the love and safety babies find in our arms.

Babywearing is not for everyone, and it's not easy at first, but I believe that all babies want to be held, and that it makes intuitive sense to hold them. Some people tell me that their babies do not want to be held, but assuming no social or sensory integration problems, evolutionary speaking, there is no advantage to *not* wanting to be held. It simply does not make sense. That being said, babies may resist a baby carrier for a variety of reasons, including hunger, exhaustion, lack of breast in mouth, need to go to the bathroom, and apprehension about a new way to be held. In addition, babies can tell when we are nervous or uncomfortable, and they often reflect our tension by resisting being held close. Babies who struggle in a baby carrier may be picking up on our anxiety or fear about the positioning and proper adjustments of a carrier, especially when we are new to babywearing.

With the right information and support, I believe that most people can have a wonderful babywearing experience with their baby. There are many organizations that can help you choose baby carriers (see the Resources section), and smaller support groups have sprung up all over the country with the exclusive purpose of helping parents wear their babies. All children eventually learn to walk and explore, and there is absolutely nothing wrong with responding to your baby's need to be held. It's intuitive and instinctual to do so. The benefits speak for themselves in my experience, since my life is easier and I am more flexible as a mom because I am a babywearer.

When I get especially worn down from all of the holding I still do, I remind myself that a small person's request and need to be held are rather simple in comparison to all of the things that they require of us: to birth them, nourish them, teach them the difference between right and wrong, explain how trees get so tall and why people have to die, and to help them become loving, kind, assertive, and sensitive people . . . all of these things are so difficult and can often seem impossibly challenging, but I will look back on all of the precious months and years of holding I did and be glad I followed my intuition, knowing that when my babies needed simply to be held, I simply held them.

6

Baby Needs Nighttime Parenting: Gentle Techniques and Co-sleeping

I have never owned a crib. Or a bassinet. We have one bedroom in our house. There are two mattresses in that bedroom. They are next to each other. One is a king-size. One is a full. We all sleep together. In one big bed.

Okay. I know you've heard of people "like us" with our family beds and our cuddling all night and thinking we are so great because we suffered through waking up every time the baby did without having them "cry it out." And we know what you think of us, so don't be coy. You wonder what the big deal is and if there is scientific proof that it's "wrong" to use cry-it-out methods or, my personal favorite term, "modified Ferber" methods (named for the original proponent of the cry-it-out method, Dr. Ferber). You wonder who sleeps where in our family bed, what it was like with a newborn, where the older kid goes and how long he'll stay there, and where my husband and I have sex. And you wonder how co-sleeping is any different from letting your kid crawl into your bed in the morning, and if you have to become a card-carrying touchy-feely hippie if you decide to co-sleep. I think that about covers it.

I know that not everyone wants a family bed or thinks it's okay to sleep with your kids. Some people want their bed to be open to their kids, but in small doses and not past a certain age. Some people don't want to adjust to a chitchatty toddler with squirmy sleep habits lying next to them. Here are some of the subtleties that helped me understand the family bed and helped us make the decision that works best for our family to get the most—and the best—sleep.

. . . .

A disclaimer:

We sleep together safely. You should co-sleep with your child only if you understand and adhere to the guidelines for safe co-sleeping.

. . . .

I did not grow up sleeping with anyone but our family cats. I had a lot of trouble sleeping as a baby, and throughout my childhood I suffered from on-and-off insomnia. I hated going to bed, I disliked being alone, I had trouble falling and staying asleep, and I had bad dreams. Sounds great, right? When my dad would go out for meetings at night, I would often "start" in my mom and dad's bed, which was a lot of fun. It was cozy and very special to chat and giggle with my mom in the darkness and have her so close to me. After I was asleep and my dad would come home, he would carry my sleeping body to my bedroom. That was the extent of my experience with the family bed.

I honestly never considered sleeping with my kids before I had them. In anthropology class in college, I learned about cultures that used a family bed, but it was not interesting to me except for the purposes of coursework. It seemed old-world: something that was done, I figured, because the cultures we were studying must not have had enough money or space for separate bedrooms or separate beds.

Before I got married, one of my friends who lived at a Zen meditation center in Northern California (not kidding) slept with her kid, and it creeped me out a little bit. Why did it creep me out? I don't know exactly. It was too intimate, too "out there," too . . . foreign. Her parents were Chinese and Portuguese, so I sort of wrote it off as something people from other countries liked to do. Soon, though, as more and more friends of mine started having kids and following their intuition, I saw that a lot of people—including those whose parents were not from other countries—slept with their kids and enjoyed the experience for a variety of reasons.

When I was pregnant with our first child, I started researching everything I could about babies, and I paid close attention to the literature on infants, children, and sleep. As I saw it, two themes emerged that I found myself investigating and confronting: 1) how a child's development dictates nighttime needs, and 2) why co-sleeping makes sense. How did I *really* feel about each of these things? Until I could be honest and get educated, I realized I was in no position to judge—or purchase a crib, for that matter.

Children's Development and Nighttime Needs

Here's the simplest way to put it: children need parenting at night as well as in the day. In the first weeks and months of life, newborns don't really know the difference between night and day. Sometimes they will have extended awake periods in the middle of the night and will sleep most of the day. And even when babies get cued in to the circadian rhythms of sleep and wake, they don't lose the need for food, closeness, comfort, or security just because the sun has gone down. They still want to wake up every few hours, nursing or not.

They still want to be reminded of your smell, your voice, and the feel of your body. Newborns cannot truly distinguish themselves from you. Their experience of the world is blurry. They are being assaulted by smells and sounds unfamiliar to them. You are home to your baby. You are what's right when everything seems wrong. You are what's right in the day, and you are also what's right in the night.

I was truly baffled by our first son's sleeping, or lack thereof (so I lamented at the time). He woke up every two hours. He would stir and eventually cry, and I did what was instinctual: I nursed him and he fell back to sleep. Sometimes this took a long time, and in the first months, it often took hours, and I was exhausted. I started having trouble staying awake during important conversations in the day, and I got sleepy at about 6:30 every night, exactly when our baby did. I fell asleep at 7 p.m. most nights in the first year, got up on average six times every night, and woke up at 7 a.m. with the baby. My social life with friends was seriously limited to short lunches and catching up by phone and email when I could. Did I mention I was really exhausted?

I investigated possible causes of this frequent and maddening night waking, which I was convinced had some specific cause. I read some conventional books, which suggested that I investigate possible allergies, such as foods I was eating or dust mites in the sheets of our bed and the percentage of polyester making its way into my son's pajamas. Then I went a more alternative approach and looked into holistic remedies for his waking. In an act of desperation, I read some sleep-training books and was told I had to come to the realization that my baby was dominating my life in a very bad way and that as soon as I admitted that, I could get him to stop waking up by consistently refusing to nurse him and respond to him. That didn't sound right to me.

Finally, I started to research sleep cycles of a baby, and I discovered that a baby's sleep cycles come in shifts of about 90 to 120 minutes, with periods of light wakeful sleep in the patterns my son had been exhibiting. Meaning: he woke up when sleep was light and he needed help going back to sleep. Some kids can get themselves back to sleep easier than others. Mine clearly was not "others." Our pediatrician confirmed this to be true, and he told me what I needed to hear and was finally ready to accept: he's waking up because he's waking up. Maybe he's hungry. Maybe he's lonely. Maybe his teeth hurt. Maybe he has to pee. Maybe he had a bad dream. Maybe he's contemplating the fact that he is a baby and would someday like to be an astronaut or a plumber. It doesn't really matter. He's waking up because he's waking up.

This may sound like a trite, ridiculous, and insane thing for a pediatrician to say, but I started talking to my friends who parented the way I wanted to, and they all said the same thing. They, too, awoke upward of four times a night on average, nursing their babies and rocking them, pacing the floors with them, and cuddling them in their arms because it was what the babies needed. These friends understood my frustration, my exhaustion, and my desperation. But they told me this: it will pass. Turn the clock to the wall. Stop counting the number of wake-ups. Just nurse and go back to sleep.

It was this advice that led to a shift in attitude that allowed me to let my son do his thing for two full years, despite my exhaustion. I would often get burnt out, and I would need a nap more often than I like to admit. I would order in food or spread out our fridge's leftovers for days to avoid having to cook a full meal because I was so tired. And sometimes I wanted it to just end. I tried once to explain to my son, when he was about eighteen months old, that I couldn't do it anymore; I was done. He cried for about one eternal minute before I realized it was the wrong thing for us to do. He needed me more than I needed sleep. It was only from consciously telling myself that I could do this, it would not go on forever, and I was not alone, that I was able to parent at night with no second thoughts and no need to let my baby cry and learn to not need me the way he believed that he did.

I decided to go without certain social activities because the commitment to this style of parenting trumped it all. Even when I struggled, I knew I would come out of it okay. I leaned heavily on friends who parented the same way, so we could complain to each other without being told: "Well, you just need to let him cry it out, and don't nurse him at night—he doesn't need it." People love to ask a new mom: "Is the baby sleeping through the night?" La Leche League meetings and my new friendships provided me with support and suggestions for how to answer, with such quips as: "Oh, he sleeps through the night, he just wakes up every two hours!" or, my personal favorite: a big, broad smile, and the word which is itself a complete sentence: "No."

I am not a superwoman. I do not have any less need for sleep than most people. I am not a special and obnoxious brand of martyr, and I do not want an award for what I do at night. However, I firmly believe that teaching your child to stop needing you at night does not teach her to not need you; rather, it teaches her that you will not respond to her needs. So let's call it what it is without any judgment: by not tending to nighttime needs, you are teaching a baby that you will not tend to their nighttime needs so they best stop asking you to. Why our culture demands this kind of independence of children who cannot even crawl, walk, talk, wipe themselves after going potty, or make a decent sandwich is beyond my understanding. Am I suggesting that you are scarring your child forever if you don't respond to nighttime needs? No. Am I suggesting that everyone can make the decision to respond all night to a baby's needs? No.

What I am saying is that I don't agree or understand parenting advice that suggests you lock *yourself* away so that you are not "tempted" to rescue your child from nights of crying it out while he is left with a distressed and largely unprepared father whose job it suddenly is to tolerate shrieking, choking on tears, and possibly throwing up from such distress, at which point baby effectively passes out and you consider this a "good night." And why, all of a sudden, do fathers become solely responsible for this difficult and often traumatic venture? I believe that just about every person has the capacity, should you desire to foster it, to adjust your nighttime needs to those of your developing infants without fear that they will never soothe themselves or will be spoiled by your attention, or that you will never have your life back. It's simply not true.

The History of Co-sleeping

For almost all of human history, people have shared a room for sleeping (called co-sleeping), if not a sleeping surface (known as bed-sharing). Now, don't get me wrong: not everything that has been done for almost all of human history needs to continue unmodified or unimproved. Take, for example, a lack of indoor plumbing, having to kill animals with your bare hands in order to eat them, or undergoing major surgery without the use of anesthesia. These things and many others, over time, have merited drastic improvement, and I, for one, am very happy we have seen progress in these areas.

However, for tens of thousands of years, human families have lived in group settings that favored sleeping together. So why the historically recent shift in sleeping arrangements? What was broken about the system that needed fixing? Turns out: not much. The practice of co-sleeping lost favorability in the same era when wealth and resources increased. As houses got bigger, there was an increased interest to separate from what were considered old-world ways. Co-sleeping was viewed as unnecessary in an environment where luxury was abundant. In addition, puritanical notions of protecting intimate arenas of life (be it nudity or simply physical closeness) combined with several rare but publicized cases of accidental smothering of a baby led to the phasing out and disdain for co-sleeping.

After learning about the history of co-sleeping and the easy and reasonable ways to safely co-sleep, I came to the honest conclusion that there is nothing to be afraid of about sleeping with one's child. It is intimate, that is true, but I can make the decision not to fear being intimate with something that careened itself out of my body and made me fall in love with it shortly thereafter. As far as I'm concerned, we're *already* pretty darn intimate. Why make arbitrary distinctions?

Downsides of Sleeping Alone: I'm Vulnerable and Lonely; How About You?

Sleeping alone leaves you vulnerable and is rarely done by most animals in nature. Picture yourself a newborn chimp, or any non-nocturnal animal for that matter. Being alone when your metabolism slows down and your body needs to rest leaves you open to attack if no one is around to defend you. Granted, we are not animals in a pure state of nature. But evolutionarily, we are much closer to animals in nature than you might like to admit. Our genetic makeup has not changed drastically enough in the tens of thousands of years since we began living in houses and communities to justify sleeping alone as beneficial in any way. We were made to sleep like animals: together.

Sleeping alone can be lonely. While it is true that children, teenagers, and adults do indeed desire and need alone time, and while it is true that many people enjoy sleeping alone, newborn babies and anyone who has ever been in love knows that sleeping next to someone feels good. It feels right. If you feel sad, there is someone there to comfort you. If you are happy, that person can share it with you. If you're cold, you can generate body heat together. If you need something, there is someone there to help you get it. And if you're a social creature (as we humans are), socializing does not end when the sun goes down. We bond at night, we talk about the day, and we process our experiences with the person who is lying next to us. And sometimes that person is very small, bald, and can't speak very well. (And no, I don't mean my husband.) By being next to a baby at night, we are sharing their experience of the world, even if we don't quite understand what that means to them yet.

I am one of those people who hates sleeping alone. I rarely crave alone time in bed, and I love nighttime closeness, which makes my husband pretty nuts. Before we had our first child, he tolerated my cuddling for a good year or so before he finally confessed that he wasn't really interested in being cuddled all night. He was fine with a good-night kiss, but after that, he was happy to roll over and not be bothered by me until the pancakes were ready the next morning.

Lucky for me, my husband studied anthropology in college, and what I learned about babies and vulnerability at night was not new to him, in his studies both of animals (specifically primates) and humans. Once I was pregnant with our first son, it was very clear to us that sleeping with him was what we wanted and needed to do, for our collective benefit. And once he was born, my husband was quite okay with me having someone to lie next to and cuddle with that wasn't him. Now he just had to deal with me tapping him on the shoulder every other hour for help with diaper changing, positioning pillows for nursing, getting me water or a snack, and, of course, so that I could point out how peaceful our boy looked while sleeping next to me.

The Upsides of Sleeping Together

Sleeping next to a newborn facilitates nursing, helps a nursing mom and dad get more rest than they would if they had to physically get up to fetch the baby from another room, allows a mother's body to regulate a baby's body temperature, and allows for complete and utter vigilance by the mother. Sleeping in close proximity to a newborn guarantees that every jumpy or erratic breath that a newborn takes is monitored by the mother (even while the mother is asleep). *Using a baby monitor is simply not the same thing as being next to your baby*. When you are physically next to them, you can feel their bodies move, you can hear and analyze subtle changes in aspiration, and you are a millisecond away from reaching out to them. Knowing that my babies were right next to me at night allowed me to rest knowing that I could tell if they were too hot, too cold, not breathing right— whatever. I felt safe next to them, and I knew they were safe next to me. I know from personal experience, after nursing every night for a combined five-plus years, that if I had to do much more than simply roll over, I think I would have truly lost my mind and seriously considered not nursing anymore. So for me, co-sleeping facilitated what turned out to be one of my best parenting tools: nursing. The way I see it, it is absolutely natural, normal, and healthy to want to be close to your newborn both day and night.

Another tremendous and, frankly, unexpected upside to co-sleeping and, in our case, bed-sharing, is that it is indescribably wonderful to sleep next to your children even if you are a light sleeper and love sleep. There is nothing that can compare to sharing sleep throughout the night, even though it takes some getting used to. Kids squirm a lot, and they often like to be pressed right up next to you for what our older son calls "the big cuddle," or they like to lie perpendicular to your body, for reasons I have never quite figured out but stopped trying to. Our older son snuggles very close for warmth at various times of the night and often has to be pried off with a surprisingly great deal of force if you need to extricate yourself from his sleepy grip.

People often assume (erroneously) that I am a heavy sleeper and that all people who co-sleep are heavy sleepers. They describe to me in gory detail how outrageously, obscenely active their kids are and how they can't deal with it because they need their sleep. First of all, I am not a heavy sleeper, so at first I felt every movement, too—but you do get used to it. And many people decide to forgo that beauty rest because they fundamentally know it is best for their baby. So you haven't convinced me you can't co-sleep yet.

Second, if you are a person who really likes sleeping, I am afraid that you will be shocked and rather disturbed to discover that *you never sleep the same way again after having kids as you did before you had them,* especially if you are a mama. You get a sort of sixth sense for your baby at night, which gets stronger if you foster it. You are programmed to instinctually seek them out when they are in distress and to be attuned to them and vigilant about them. Many people wish this instinct would go away so they could just get some good sleep. Sorry, folks. That instinct is helpful and serves to keep your baby safe.

And finally, there is no way to describe the feeling of intermittently waking up to your child's little body curled up next to you throughout the night as you yourself make your journey through the stages of light sleep: little voices whispering their dreams, emitting sweet baby smells from their soft skin and silky hair, stretching with tender little arms and legs that you remember used to be so tiny ("Wasn't it just yesterday that they were born?" you may find yourself wondering in the dark of night). Their limbs are so strong all day, but at night, they seem so delicate, splayed out in hysterical and impossible contortions. Little lips reach out for kisses and spontaneously proclaim their love for you at night as in day, and as soon as their language catches up to their contented hearts that have known since you first held them that, indeed, they loved you, they will tell you.

So What Does a Marriage Look Like with the Family Bed?

I already told you about our two beds, but we actually started with one. I brought to our marriage a lovely and expensive full-size Japanese futon on a fancy black wooden platform. (My husband brought a single mattress on a wire frame that went straight to Goodwill.) We slept on the futon on the platform until we had our first son, at which point we simply decided not to worry that our baby might fall off the bed by taking away the platform and putting the mattress directly on the floor. Did it sacrifice the aesthetics of our bed? Yes. Did it look a little bit like we were staying in a youth hostel while on a five-week tour of Spain? A little bit, yes. Do you *have* to sleep on the floor if you co-sleep? No. Nothing makes me cringe more than someone telling me co-sleeping "doesn't work" because their second cousin's best friend's teacher's plumber's kid fell out of the bed. It gives co-sleeping a bad name if you have a child in your bed without protecting him from falling out of it! There are many simple, inexpensive, and discreet modifications to your bed, such as bumpers or attachments that can allow you to safely co-sleep.

We slept with our first son in our futon on the floor very happily (and very cozily) for two years. When I got pregnant with our second son, we upgraded to a king-size futon and cleared a space in our one bedroom for the full-size to abut it. I began sleeping with our older son on the "big boy" bed, and my husband gradually began taking over his nighttime needs as he weaned and my pregnancy progressed. Once the baby came, the baby slept with me on the king-size, and my husband slept with our older son on the full.

In the early months after the baby arrived, our older son was pretty distraught, and I often slept with both boys; one on either side of me. Within a year of the baby's birth, my husband and my older son's book time and together time in the evenings made my husband the preferred sleeping pal for our older son. One night a week I make a point to have both boys in the bigger bed, but I often awaken to see that our older son has silently crawled back to my husband, where he lies contentedly smooshed in his father's arms.

The question I get a lot is about me and my husband. And the sex. The people who ask are usually the people who also had more sex than we did *before* we had kids, but I understand the interest nonetheless. My husband happens to have come to the conclusion that bed-sharing is the best thing for our family. It fosters closeness, intimacy, and secure attachment, and this from a guy who hates cuddling at night. It feels good and it feels right. I am blessed to have a husband who agrees that this is ideal for us, even though he did not grow up with this concept.

Does that mean he doesn't desire to *not* have our boys in the bed sometimes? Sure. He wants to sleep in most days but rarely gets to. Our boys sleep in our bed. And we don't get to have sex in it. And that's the long and the short of it. We can be intimate in any other room of the house. And we have done just that. I am aware (and he is, too) that this is not the most convenient way to have intimacy. It's also not always the most comfortable way to have intimacy. But we have collectively and consciously chosen to live our life this way right now. There are worse things in life and in relationships.

I assume that if we had our bed to ourselves, we would have more sex. But a lot of couples I talk to who parent this way have less sex than they did before anyway, and that's also okay. Not everything is the same when you have kids as when you didn't have them. Things change, priorities change, schedules change. We are rolling with the punches. I value my husband's needs greatly. I value our marriage and want it to be secure and enduring. I want our boys to see a model of a couple that communicates, helps each other, and loves to be a family together. That is what I need to focus on; not that I am having less sex than before I had kids and not that I am having less sex than my friends who don't have a family bed. My husband and I believe that we need to follow our instincts. And if you feel a desire to be with your children at night like we do, you will try to figure out how to work everything else in around that.

In Conclusion

I don't know if there is a topic more hotly discussed than getting babies to sleep the way we want them to. People spend thousands of dollars on books, gadgets, CDs, and expensive sleep trainers to coerce a tiny helpless creature into growing up, gaining independence, and being able to self-soothe and put herself to sleep. I decided to surrender a little bit and dive under the wave of my kids' nighttime needs instead of trying to jump over the wave. The wave was way over my head, anyway, and sometimes my best assessment is right: this was not a fight I was going to win easily. So I gave up the fight and was happier, better rested, and more fun to be around, both day and night.

I know that co-sleeping and bed-sharing are not for everyone, but there may be some helpful aspects of the concepts even if you can't imagine the application in your home. First, know that your child expresses needs, not manipulations. If your child indicates that he is not ready to be alone at night, do whatever works for you to encourage nighttime independence (if that's what you seek to foster), but try not to discourage your child from expressing his feelings. Resist parenting by "fear": fear that your child will never be able to fall asleep without you, fear that he will never leave your bed or your bedroom if you give in. Parent by intuition, not fear.

Second, don't be afraid of the intimacy that sleeping near your child facilitates. It is okay to cuddle your child and to enjoy the warmth you feel in your heart when you hold your little one close. There is nothing to be ashamed of, even if you carefully select who you choose to tell about your nighttime sleeping arrangements.

And finally, be open to trying new things if there are struggles surrounding sleep. Fighting with your child about nighttime needs will likely encourage more fighting about them. Decide what is important to you and work toward it gently and with an open mind. You never know what solutions your child may come up with that will work for you.

As for us, our son eventually learned to sleep at night, all night. We choose to lie with him until he falls asleep, but that is showing signs of shifting as he gains confidence and we let him explore how that looks and feels. Children who share sleep with their parents tend not to fear the night, and they do not fear sleep.

The family bed is the place where we are all equal, and after our second son was born, I believe it was the family bed that made the world right for our older son. We are all equal when our eyes are closed and when we hold one another. Even though the baby needed nursing and pottying and pacing and so much more of me than our older son could bear to give up, when we turned off the lights, our breath became one huge sigh of relief, exhaustion, and tenderness. And we slept until morning.

Our boys will outgrow the family bed, and they will most likely sleep together in a sibling bed, or in bunk beds when the time is right for them both. It will be sometime between now and before they graduate high school when this occurs. It is normal for children to want independence, but much of that is determined by peer pressure and by influences of the media as to what is "normal" for a child. Our sons don't think that anyone should sleep alone. It baffles their minds to contemplate it. This may sound like they are naive, but we think it's lovely.

Sleep ought to be the place where children are safe and tended to, and the way we choose to parent them should depend not on the location of the sun or the moon in the sky, but on the basic and simple needs and desires of their bodies and souls.

7

Baby Needs Potty:
Elimination Communication

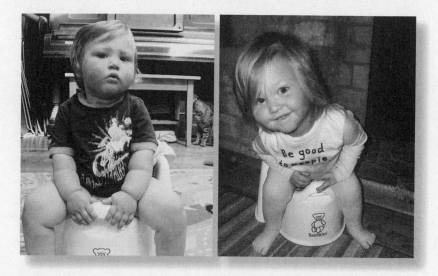

How did I avoid potty-training either of my boys? Easy! Babies are *born* potty-trained; it's the *parents* who need the training! I would not be surprised if you flipped straight to this chapter to satisfy your curiosity, or perhaps just for a chuckle at my expense—and with good reason: the subject of potty-training children is loaded, controversial, and oftentimes incredibly frustrating. In addition, potty-training is sometimes the most difficult experience people report in their first years of being a parent, one that is often a miserable and disheartening emotional minefield. And here's why: the battle is between you and a person much shorter and far less cognitively developed than you who can outsmart, outreason and outwit you incredibly easily.

So how did I escape this battle, and is there anything I can offer you that is of value even if you don't want to put your newborn on a potty?

This all started when I was pregnant with my first son. I met a woman through a mutual friend who was also pregnant. We got to talking, and she said she was having a stressful pregnancy because, upon deciding to practice "elimination communication" (also known as natural infant hygiene), she needed to pull up all of the carpets in her home before the baby arrived so that she would be ready on day one to start. That's not all. She went on to tell me that she was living in a tent in her backyard while this was being done. Very pregnant. In a tent. In her backyard. So that she could have a diaper-free baby. And her in-laws were questioning her sanity. Um . . . yeah, I was questioning her sanity, too! This new acquaintance and I ended up having our children on the exact same day, and we became very close friends in the coming months. Aside from my feeling that she was underhandedly trying to outdo my earthiness (aren't cloth diapers enough of an out-of-the-box statement?), she and I shared a lot of holistic and progressive philosophies and tendencies, and it was wonderful to have a buddy with whom to share fears, excitement, and complaints about adjusting to life with a high-needs in-arms newborn.

To be quite frank, I avoided asking her about how elimination communication (EC, as it is commonly known) was going for her and her daughter, since it really sounded so absolutely crazy to me that I was afraid to get her talking about it, lest I be unable to hold back my disdain and skepticism. However, she was unable *not* to talk about it, and she sang the praises of the connection and em-powerment she felt. I listened politely, but then one day, when our babies were almost six months old, she handed me one of the classic books written on the subject. I begrudgingly accepted it with a weak smile. I was doing a lot of sitting around in those days and weeks and months, though, nursing and having the baby snooze on me for hours on end, so more out of boredom than curiosity, I read it.

To put it lightly, I was fascinated. I was moved. I agreed with the philosophies put forth in the book more than I wanted to admit; philosophies about a baby's needs, desires, and rights, and about the planet and our responsibility both to our baby and to our baby's world. All of it just made sense.

When people ask me if my husband has been on board with all of the parenting choices we make, I usually reply that we arrived at almost all of our decisions together. EC is the one thing I proposed, though, that he found totally ridiculous, completely unnecessary, and more than a little bit insane. When I first told my husband about it, I began, "What would you think if I told you that everything we have been told about babies and diapers was actually all a sham?" He stared at me blankly. I continued. I was all fired up and ready to educate my ignorant husband about the pitfalls of not just disposable diapers but any diapers at all: "Babies are born knowing they need to go to the bathroom! They don't *want* to go in their pants! It would save this country millions of dollars and we could decrease the landfills and we would bond with our baby in ways we never dreamed possible if we just *help him use a potty instead of diapers*! He will train *us*! We'll have a diaper-free baby! ISN'T THIS EXCITING?" He stared blankly again. He was not excited. Not at all. Not even a little bit.

And my husband is not alone. I know that most people think that EC is really out there, totally impossible, and also a good dose of silly. I believe, though, that even if EC is not for you, there is something of value to be learned from hearing why we do it, how we do it, and what the benefits are. And even if you still think it's out there, impossible, and truly very, very silly, you can still take something from it that may help when you do eventually potty-train your toddler.

The Theory

Forget what you think you know just for a few paragraphs. Babies are born with an innate sense of their bodies. Within days of birth, most newborns make reliable, if subtle, indications of when they need to go to the bathroom. These signals vary from baby to baby, but with reinforcement, babies will learn quite quickly to make stronger, more overt, and more reliable signals when the need arises.

If you, the parent, make the commitment to learn your baby's signals, you can significantly reduce—or eliminate—the amount of diapers you use, because *your baby will train you* to take her to the bathroom when she needs to use it. Babies can communicate their elimination needs to you. This is the essence of EC.

Here are a few important things to know about EC.

EC is not potty-training.

EC is not about making babies do something they don't want to do. There is no reward or punishment. We do not clap or hold up "touchdown arms" when a baby successfully uses the toilet; we do not make charts with little gold stars, and we do not bribe with sweets. We do not scold or get angry with a baby who poops on the floor or uses the diaper instead of the toilet. Those of us who practice EC see it as a sort of Zen experience: attachment to any outcome— positive or negative—is bound to disappoint, so we simply observe behavior and take note of what works or doesn't work for our baby on any given day or at any developmental stage. Babies instinctively do not want to eliminate in a diaper, just as animals in nature do not want to eat or sleep in the same place in which they have eliminated. In this country and many others, *we are essentially teaching our children to go to the bathroom in a diaper,* and then fighting with them and sometimes chastising them in the name of "potty-training" some two, three, four, and (in a more recent, startling trend) often five or six years later.

You need to be around your baby a lot to reliably learn his/her signals.

If signals are not reinforced, a baby will stop making them. Since signals change with age and developmental stages, learning your baby's signals once does not guarantee EC "success." Constant contact with your child ensures that you can observe them, learn their patterns, and reinforce their signals consistently. This allows you to communicate with them on a completely nonverbal level about their bathroom needs. And EC is not just for moms. Other caregivers, such as dads, grandparents, nannies, and babysitters can also participate. Many babies are thrilled to have more than one caregiver meet their EC needs.

Disposable diapering is a multibillion-dollar industry.

The famous 1962 study that stated that children are not "toilet ready" until they are verbal was authored by pediatrician T. Berry Brazelton, who sat on the Pampers Parenting Institute Pediatric Roundtable and has personally advertised diapers sized for *six-year-olds*. The 1999 "Updated Review" published in *Pediatrics* was sponsored by Procter & Gamble, the largest producer of disposable diapers (Pampers) in the world. You don't have to be a holistic mama to know that this sounds fishy.

Much of the world practices (or has practiced) EC.

Many African, Asian, and Middle Eastern women still practice EC. They don't call it EC. They call it normal. In cultures where babies are frequently carried on a mother's body, the mother learns very quickly to identify the squirming (as well as other signals) that precedes a baby going to the bathroom. Although sanitation is often a contributing factor to a particular culture's need to not use diapers, most non-Westerners are astounded that, statistically, Americans struggle to keep women breastfeeding past six months but keep children in diapers well over two or three years. In most countries, it is the opposite.

EC is a lot of work, but it is worth it.

It is far easier in the first two years of your child's life to encourage him to go to the bathroom in his diaper rather than take him to the bathroom all the time. However, I am certain that it is far more difficult to negotiate with and potty-train a two-, three-, four-, five-, or six-year-old than it is to have a twelve-month-old use the American Sign Language–designated sign for "bathroom," crawl or walk to a potty unassisted, wear underwear, and have no conscious memory of ever fighting with a caregiver about where, when, or how to *not* go to the bathroom.

Vocabulary

Potty (n,v): the receptacle for elimination (an infant potty, grown-up toilet, bucket, empty ten-gallon ice-cream container, any kitchen mixing bowl, or foliage and bushes anywhere they and an EC child are found); the act of helping a child eliminate in such a receptacle.

Pee/poop (n,v): elimination from a baby consisting of very dilute and very sanitary urine from the urethra in females or in males, or very (in an exclusively breastfed baby) odorless, thin, and easy to clean up by-product of the intestines and the colon; the act of helping a child eliminate in such a way.

Catch (n,v): elimination *not* in a diaper; the act of helping a child eliminate *not* in a diaper.

Miss (n,v): elimination in a diaper, on the floor, on your shirt, all over your poor husband's shirt, pants, boxer shorts, socks, and shoes as he is walking out the door for work, on the bedsheets, on your mother-in-law, etc.; the act of not getting a child to a potty in time.

Potty strike (n): situation where a baby for a variety of known and/or unknown reasons refuses to use any potty for a day, week, or month, preferring instead to use a diaper or whatever surface or fabric is directly beneath the groin area. Aka *very frustrating*.

The Reluctant Husband and What It Looked Like

After listening to my husband's objections to trying EC, I started to doubt myself about the whole thing. He said it was going to be too much work. *He was probably right,* I sighed. He said it would be too messy. *Not if I have good success!* I thought. He said it would put distance between him and the baby because he wouldn't be able to hold him without being peed or pooped on. He was upset. This made me pause. He was indicating what I knew to be true: I already had a leg up on the bond with the baby because of breastfeeding, and he didn't want to feel *more* left out. And let's face it: no one really wants to be peed or pooped on by a baby. As a compromise, I told him that I would put a diaper on the baby whenever he was holding him, but that I wanted to give this EC thing a shot. So I did.

With my son almost six months old, I was at the upper end of what is commonly suggested as the critical period for initiating EC. I began by simply observing when he went to the bathroom. I dressed him in a cotton prefold diaper loosely slung about him, and I kept checking to see when it got wet. I saw a pattern: about every fifteen minutes, he peed, bless his little heart. He liked to go to the bathroom after nursing (who wouldn't?) and sometimes while nursing (no comment). He peed every two hours all night just before I nursed him, and then he would start this routine all over again. I was intimidated. Every fifteen minutes!? Okay, I already didn't have *much* of a life, but this would seriously cut into what was left of it!

What gave me hope and started to turn my husband around was that our baby was absolutely giving signs. He would flap his arms up and down as if attempting to take flight (we called it the "wing flap" and even made up a little ditty about it), and when we tried to pee him (see verb form of "pee" in glossary above), he went. Amazing. My husband was a believer.

By twelve months, for the most part, that baby of ours would not pee in a diaper. He used the potty. He learned the ASL sign for "potty" by ten months. At the parent-and-me class we started attending when he was thirteen months old, the teacher stared at me, mouth agape, as I told her that he can't talk, he can't walk, and he hasn't yet eaten solid food, but he can tell me when he needs to go to the bathroom. I can count on one hand the number of poopy diapers he had since he was eight months old. Everything went into the potty. By eighteen months, he was wearing underwear. He has no conscious memory of ever peeing or pooping in a diaper.

What was occurring was that our baby's signals became stronger and patterns emerged (timing is often helpful when signals are not being used as much as they usually are). You really, truly can learn your baby's elimination cues. Once children learn to use the potty, they don't "hold" it, they wait until they are in a position that is familiar and comfortable for them. It's not just that they like to pee when you take their diaper off. They really learn to use the potty. They don't get urinary-tract infections and it's not unhealthy. And believe me: if they really need to go, they'll go anywhere. And I mean *anywhere.*

Speaking of anywhere, it's best not to leave a baby diaper-free in a carpeted room, and any time you are not in the mood to be vigilant, please put a diaper on your baby! They don't know which furniture is expensive; they are equal-opportunity soilers. In all honesty, some people cannot imagine a baby's pee or poop anywhere but in a diaper, but just as we make small adjustments to our expectations about what our home will look like with a baby (by removing breakables from within reach of little hands, for example), so we can, with a little preparation, make our homes safe for baby to be around—diaper or not.

EC babies are typically held up with their behind to your tummy over toilets, sinks, and yes, bushes and trees. They are held propped up on infant potties, of which there are many models available. When they are old enough, they can sit up on their own and will eventually crawl and walk to the potty. You can EC at night as well as in the day; some people use cloth diapers to catch misses, and others (purists) lay out bedding that can be laundered easily if there is a miss. We use an EC belt (picture a giant hair scrunchy around baby's waist) with a prefold tucked in (picture a two-foot-tall sumo wrestler and that's what our guys mostly looked like for the first years of their lives). Most EC-ers use cloth diapers, so that misses are felt by the baby; it is this sense of wetness that you want to allow so that the baby learns that it feels better to use a potty rather than one's diaper. Once a child starts eating solids, it is easier to read signs for pooping (as any EC or non-EC parent can tell you!), and you will be simultaneously astounded and thrilled at what *can* come out of a small person's body and what does not necessarily *need* to go into a diaper for you to subsequently attempt to clean up.

It's not a perfect science. We have had our share of misses, and we have endured the sneers of folks who saw those misses and nodded contentedly: "I just *knew* it couldn't really work!" More often than not, we shrugged it off and were grateful for all of our catches. When a baby is sick or teething, her signals are not always consistent. A child who arches her back when you attempt to potty her does not want to use the potty even if you think she does. Even very young babies are sensitive to our moods, and they often refuse to eliminate when we are rushing them or otherwise stressed.

These are great lessons in parenting, not just pottying: you get to do things your way. Let others say what they will. You know your baby better than anyone. Some days are better than others, and your baby will never fail to amaze you by calling you out on it. It's as if he is saying, "Having a rough day? Sorry, but please don't take it out on me, or I won't pee in this potty. I'll pee on the rug." A point well taken.

The Result

The benefits of EC are numerous. What I report here is by no means unusual; it is the norm for those who make the commitment to EC. With our second son, we started EC on day two. By the time he was two weeks of age, we had to pinch ourselves when two patterns became clear to both my husband and me: 1) the baby would refuse to nurse when he had to go to the bathroom, and 2) he got a weird far-off gaze when he had to go.

It is worth noting that starting EC early does not alter a child's overall development. That is to say, learning is not accelerated by practicing EC, and you simply cannot teach a three-month-old to use the ASL sign for potty, nor can you teach a four-month-old to walk to a potty and pull their little tiny underpants down. That kind of motor development still happens only when it normally would. So starting early means fewer diapers but it does not mean a totally toilet-independent baby. Tiny EC babies still need a lot of your help.

Despite these caveats, starting so early with our second son worked for us and it worked for him, too. He gave strong signals from very early on and has been dry for the majority of his life. He started to use the ASL sign when he was just under a year old (a bit later than his brother, which is not unusual for a second child) and was in tiny underwear by fifteen months, before he could even walk. We have had more misses with him than we did with our first son, since most of our time is spent with both boys to take care of. The luxury of two-on-one vigilance and, thus, the success that we had with our first son in catching every signal or every pee is not as possible, but we have still been truly amazed by this process.

The incredible upsides to EC are:

Potty green!

Less diaper usage means less waste (disposable diapers account for one third of nonbiodegradable content in landfills), less laundry (if you are a cloth family), more money in your pocket (we did not buy diapers or pay a diaper service after our boys turned twelve months!).

Pee and poop are not gross when they are your baby's.

Our culture's obsession with cleanliness and sanitary measures that seek to foster bacteria- and germ-free environments puts distance between you and your newborn, who often needs to be tended to in the most intimate ways. EC allows you to demystify the inner workings of your baby by putting you in touch with and in control of his elimination patterns. This is not just hippie-dippie mumbo jumbo. Knowing what is "normal" elimination allows you to identify when things are not normal, as in cases of sickness, infection, and even benign changes in elimination that result from teething. An EC-ing friend of mine noticed a tiny amount of blood in her son's urine one morning that would not have been detectable had he been using a diaper. She took him to the pediatrician, who confirmed that he had the very start of a urinary-tract infection. Her early detection eliminated the need for antibiotics, since she was able to treat the first symptoms on her own. At that moment, she felt so empowered and blessed to be an EC parent. Why not be the expert on all aspects of your baby? You intuitively know best what your baby needs, and knowing about his elimination is an empowering and wonderful parenting tool to have.

Diaper rash, be gone!

Guess what? EC children do not get diaper rash. Diaper rash is caused by a child sitting in urine and feces. Once we began EC with our older son, he never had diaper rash again. Our younger son has *never* had diaper rash—ever. Aside from the inconvenience of diaper rash for the parents, it is painful for the baby. Treatments for diaper rash are either steroid-based (in severe cases) or are simply barriers against moisture building up on the skin. Disposable-diaper companies have responded by making more and more "absorbent" diapers with the selling point that your child never feels wet. Not only does extra absorbency mean added chemicals that are not always safe or thoroughly tested, this Band-Aid attempt at a solution strikes me as bizarre. Put very simply: children should not have to sit in their own waste. When friends ask me how to treat diaper rash, I respond that the best solution is to keep wet or poopy diapers off the child's skin until it goes away. They are usually repulsed at the notion of having to deal with pee or poop. Even if dealing with it for a day would take away cracked and bleeding skin? I repeat: pee and poop are not gross when they are your baby's. Really.

I parent better because of EC.

This is the one people love to hear about. As I mentioned, my kids started to speak really late. My older son did not speak sentences until he was over three years old. There's nothing "wrong" with him, and my younger son is on track to speak even later than his older brother. It's just how my kids come out: big, slow-moving, mellow, and quiet. A dear friend of mine with a daughter the same age as my son would often marvel at how well I understood my first son before he was verbal. She noticed that I maintained a complete and total connection with him regarding all of his needs: nursing, eating, mood shifts, discomfort, and even teething. She was right; I knew the meaning to every expression he made, every shoulder shrug, every head-on-my-shoulder, every frown. She couldn't figure out how this happened for us and why he was rarely frustrated with his inability to talk, even when all of his peers did. Then she did EC with her second daughter, and she said that she received the gift she had seen me receive: EC helped her communicate globally on a deeper level with her daughter.

How EC Can Help You Even if You Don't Want to Do It

Assuming you have stayed with me this far, you probably think I have nothing better to do than hold a newborn over a bucket and then stand on a soapbox about how I understand my kids perfectly because we practiced EC. Don't worry: I know that EC is not for everyone. It's actually not for most people, and that's fine. For our family, this practice has revolutionized what we thought our parenting could be, and that's what I think is universal to all parents, whether they EC or not. The investment and effort we put in when our children are little—no matter how we parent—affects them and us for the rest of their lives. EC is one investment we stand behind (no pun intended) all the way, but I think that the outcomes of EC can be used by parents even if they potty-train the conventional way.

When you decide to potty-train, remember that the connection you forge with a child whose needs are completely, totally, and 100 percent taken care of is remarkable. There is nothing about our kids that is too intimate, too gross, or too challenging for us to learn and master. This is true no matter when your child learns to use the potty. Once we have a deep and profound understanding of our children, they will know that they are truly understood.

By starting EC with our younger son as a newborn, I have gained a new appreciation for understanding elimination, since behaviors I had dismissed with our first son as fussing or clinginess have turned out to be clear and reliable signs that he needs to use the potty. We have been amazed at how much of a child's behavior is—we believe—actually related to elimination needs. So no matter when you potty-train your children, it's great to keep in mind that the need to use the bathroom can affect them in a lot of ways, and it's always safe to be gentle as you embark on this journey.

Truth be told, for my husband, seeing that he did not have to scrape adult-size and adult-odored poop off of a talking, walking, and sometimes moody and volatile toddler's bottom was the greatest benefit and reward for our early hard work and commitment to EC. My previously skeptical husband, who was incredibly annoyed with me even mentioning the idea of EC, is now a tremendous believer in both the practice and the philosophy, so much so that I have heard him—indeed, a very involved, hands-on father, but by no means a touchy-feely "I love talking about my baby's poop" kind of guy— encouraging pregnant couples we know to consider EC. As wide-eyed strangers more concerned with a safe and easy labor than how to catch newborn poop in a bucket stare blankly at him, I smile to myself. I know that stare. I have been on both ends of that stare. And I intuitively know for sure that babies are born potty-trained. It's up to us to get with the program.

Part III

What Baby Doesn't Need

8

Baby Doesn't Need All That Stuff:
Figuring Out the Essentials

A few years ago, I went to make a return at a large national chain store that sells a little bit of everything. In one stop, you can buy toilet paper, gardening supplies, clothing, greeting cards, candy, and—yes: baby things.

I must have been there at the exact hour when all of the other moms arrived, because I saw no fewer than eight moms with children under the age of one as I walked around the store that day. Ever the amateur anthropologist, I felt that something was not quite right to me about all of these mom-and-baby duos. I figured it out very quickly: *stuff*.

Each of these moms was loaded up with stuff: expensive strollers with fancy satin-lined blankets tucked around the baby; elaborate car-seat carriers with several dangling, and even sometimes electric, toys; and decorative pacifiers on hand-stitched pacifier holders. If not in a stroller or car seat, the baby sat in one of those huge fabric shopping-cart seat inserts, lest a hand and body part touch the metal of the cart—and all of the germs implied to be lurking thereon.

What was equally disturbing to me, though, was discovering the contents of the shopping carts and baskets these moms had: more stuff. Stuff for babies. Stuff for tiny babies and medium-sized babies and older babies. Just stuff. Lots and lots of stuff.

Now, you may be thinking that I am being too quick to judge. Perhaps all of the stuff in their carts is gifts for friends or needy people who have no money to buy their children this stuff. And you may very well be right. But let's just say for the sake of argument that this stuff I saw in their carts was indeed theirs. And if I am wrong, and all that stuff wasn't for their baby, well, then somewhere in America, in some large chain store, there *is* a mom with a cart full of stuff for *her* baby. So let's go from there.

Kinds of Stuff

In this country and many others, there is a huge market for selling and distributing stuff for babies. It is a multibillion-dollar industry worldwide. There is, one might say, an obscene embarrassment and abundance of stuff available for babies. I am not naive to the ways of the free market: people demand stuff, so the industry supplies it. If no one wanted to buy all of this stuff, it would not be bought, and companies would stop making it. But people *do* want to buy all of this stuff. And we don't seem to be tiring of buying—in some cases, as much as we possibly can. So it keeps being generated for babyhood, toddlerhood, childhood, and beyond.

- There is stuff to hold a baby: bouncy seats, semistationary play stations that feature a variety of toys, bells and whistles, and tiny little chairs for babies too young to support their torsos unassisted.
- There is stuff to give a baby movement: strollers, vibrating bouncy seats, cloth bucket seats suspended by elastic bungeelike ropes, and electric battery-powered swings.
- There is layette stuff: elaborate and often very high-priced clothing, shoes—for babies who can't even walk!—fancy blankets, crib bumpers, fitted and flat crib sheets, crib bed skirts, and a variety of pillows, all in coordinating fabrics.
- And there is electric stuff: baby monitors (sound only, video screen only, or both), stuffed animals implanted with devices that simulate the sound of a human heartbeat, and baby-wipe warmers.

Perhaps the largest category of stuff consists of the thousands upon thousands of things created for newborns and babies just for use in the first year of life. This stuff includes toys and books that are specifically designed (or so we are told) to "stimulate" a baby's brain, and many of them sing, beep, whistle, and talk.

Frankly, I don't think we need any of it.

It is my belief—and many parents interested in a more natural parenting style agree—that we intuitively know how to play with our babies in their first year. In fact, you probably already possess almost everything a baby needs in that first year.

What's Wrong with Stuff?

Newborns have very specific needs. They need nourishment, vigilant care, and closeness. As they leave newbornhood and enter babyhood (somewhere around four months), their consciousness begins to expand, as do their motor skills. They eventually sit up unassisted and learn to grasp things in their hands. It is developmentally critical that babies be given stimulation so that their brains and bodies can develop appropriately. It is our job as parents to oversee this development, and much of this is intuitive.

This is the stage when manufacturers of stuff step in. They want to sell us so much cute stuff, and we spend a lot of our time trying to get our baby to be interested in the stuff we have so lovingly selected or received from well-meaning and generous family and friends. Sometimes babies are fascinated by stuff. They will swat at stuff, smile at stuff, put stuff in their gummy, drooling mouths, and they may even show preferences for some stuff over other stuff.

However, this attention to certain items does not replace *you* and your presence and attention as your baby's favorite and best-designed stuff.

That's right. Just you, as you are. No training necessary. Just intuition. There is no stuff that can replace holding your baby, taking walks with your baby, and talking to your baby about what you see and think and feel. Your baby will be entranced by you singing to him and allowing him to witness you living life: going to the market, getting the mail, cooking, interacting with other children and adults. You are the best stuff around. No question about it.

Now, even the most devoted and committed intuitive parents can hardly imagine spending all of their waking and sleeping hours with their baby with no breaks. Enter stuff. It is our hope that stuff exists that can give us a break. And with the best of intentions, we seek out stuff. We of course plan to still give them undivided attention when they are playing with their stuff, but we all know that we get exhilarated at the thought of having our hands free to check email, cook, or do things we want to do that do not involve playing with or entertaining a baby.

However, babies will make it clear to you that they want you and not stuff. They usually do this in one of two ways: 1) after feeling ignored or getting bored, they will subsequently get fussy and noisy, or 2) after becoming so entranced (hypnotized, some might suggest) by the distractions their stuff provides, they become withdrawn and silent. The break you get may be liberating for a portion of your time, but either outcome is a sign that your baby needs more from you. Your baby needs you—not stuff. One of the ways your baby will become securely attached to you is through your play together—that valuable face time you give your young child. Babies need to feel your presence for the majority of their young lives, and stuff can simply get in the way.

What Stuff *Should* Babies Have?

There is nothing inherently wrong with stuff for your baby, and it is fun and helpful to buy it. But what you may not realize is that babies don't need an abundance of stuff to play with or choose from. Babies can be kept very happy and stimulated with, for example, common household items rotated to maintain their interest. And fortunately for us, their long-term memory for stuff is alarmingly undeveloped in the first years of life!

I have found that the best toys for small babies are simple and inexpensive. For example, our boys loved cups, bowls, spoons, pots and pans, a large baby mirror, and brightly colored string (only when monitored to prevent accidental strangling or ingestion). We chose to spend more money on a few choice items in order to get quality, long-lasting, and nontoxic stuff, such as wooden stacking bowls, a wooden teething ring, and a few simple fabric books, puppets, and dolls. (Note: Babies don't really need a lot of books at first, but they will enjoy hearing your voice read to them from very early on.)

We do not own toys with batteries. If we receive them as gifts, we either donate them or we let the batteries run out and do not replace them. We simply tell our sons, "Looks like the batteries ran out!" and they stare at us for a second and then just keep on playing. We make clear to family and friends that we prefer wooden toys and don't need a lot of stuff in our lives. Several friends of ours have drafted gentle and loving letters to their families during birthdays and the holiday season, and many of us donate gifts to charities rather than keep accumulating stuff.

Is our house the perfect portrait of wooden toys and harmonious natural fiber dolls? Not at all. Some toys do not exist in wood, and our older son really feels a strong need for a lot of Lego as well as enough fire engines for a "five-alarm fire." However, the discipline and the concept are valuable to us, even if there is a shift in them every once in a while as our world expands. We just know that we can't and won't let it expand to include too much stuff.

What Does Stuff Teach Us and Our Kids?

I know I sound like a party pooper. I'm not. The habits we demonstrate when our children are babies and toddlers invariably set the stage for what their lives will look like as they get older.

The way I see it, acquiring a lot of stuff inherently implies that the world has unlimited resources and that our job is to consume those resources. Shel Silverstein's *The Giving Tree* was my first lesson in the limits to the planet's resources, and it is as profound for us today as it was thirty years ago. Our planet cannot tolerate us consuming this way anymore, and the culture our children will contribute to as they mature past babyhood cannot, either.

The almost obsessive compulsion to buy everything we want and to have more than we need encourages older children both to follow our lead in consuming and to identify themselves by the stuff that they have, rather than the people they are underneath all the stuff. If we shape our identity around what we have, how much money we spend on it, and how much more we can acquire, children will take note of that and may start to have disdain for those who do not have what they do. We would like to think our kids will be exquisitely sensitive to financial disparity in the world, but I am afraid that for the most part, they may not be.

One thing we do to severely decrease our sons' desire for stuff is not to allow them to watch television or see movies. It may sound bizarre and inconvenient. Or it may sound really appealing to you. After all, imagine how much more time you would be with your kids if they did not watch television! But one of the primary tools—if not *the* primary tool—of the stuff industry is to advertise to children, largely during television time.

Children who watch commercials are inundated with images and messages about what stuff they need, and anyone whose child has watched television knows that they desire a lot of stuff relating to their favorite television shows and characters. Clothing, books, games, toys, and electronics are all designed with the intent of satisfying your children's desire for stuff with their favorite character on it. And it's easy to get sucked in. By limiting media—at least in some amount—you take back some control by limiting the pressure on your child from the stuff industry.

Is my zero-tolerance method of TV and movies the only way to go? Absolutely not. Will I be able to maintain this ban as my kids get older? Obviously, I won't have as much control over what they do when they leave our house and visit their friends in a few years. But for now, it's the guideline that works well for us, and I really do see a difference in how my kids relate to stuff and the world around them. I don't know if it will last forever. But honestly, I feel great that right now stuff isn't getting in our way.

What Does Limiting Stuff Teach Us and Our Kids?

Limiting stuff shows respect for the earth and its resources. By making conscious choices about what stuff we have, we reduce the mark we leave on the earth, and we show the ultimate earth-friendly gesture of consuming less. Although you may think that your children are too young to be concerned with this, the earlier we start modeling kindness to the earth, the more it becomes an effortless part of our commitment to protect the earth and its resources. Limiting stuff is a great way to start.

Limiting stuff encourages self-control. When we want something, we need to weigh many things: how much it costs, how badly we want it, and ultimately, is it necessary? This forces a stricter definition of "need" that is not simply the fulfillment of a desire but a contemplation of where we put our resources. Children learn very early about what is theirs and what is not; how much gentler it would be for our communities and our planet if children showed a knowledge of control of their desires when it may not be what is best for the greater number.

Limiting stuff helps us have more money to spend on the things we need, since we do not use our money for every fleeting desire. There should always be room for us to spend on things we want and things that bring us joy, but most of the spending we do, especially when we are parents, ought to be first and foremost on necessities. When we demonstrate frugality, it sends a message to our children that we care about what we spend money on and value wise decisions that allow for flexibility and security.

So Long, Stuff

We still see how the desire for stuff makes its way into our homes, and if I could eliminate all of the advertisements from newspapers that appear for the months preceding the winter holidays every year, I would. Those months are truly difficult for me, since I did not grow up with a tradition of pointing out the stuff I wanted to my parents; that option did not exist in a family where money was not in surplus.

I tell our sons that our family makes decisions about what we purchase and that money is for the things we need as well as the things we want. I remind our boys of this when we go to toy stores, and for the most part, it goes well. However, the sadness I feel when I cannot buy everything my sons want is not only for their pain (no matter how insignificant I may find it). It is also for children whose desires will never be met, kids for whom there is never a time when their needs for food, clean water, medicine, clothing, and shoes—their most basic necessities—are met.

Have faith that you intuitively know how to parent your baby, not only to care for her most basic necessities, but also to care for her creative, intellectual, and motor development. This happens not with things *made* for your baby; this happens because *you* were made for your baby.

9

Baby Doesn't Need Unnecessary Medical Intervention: When (and When Not) to Call the Doctor

When you are blessed with a child, it is truly an awesome and awe-inspiring event worthy of gratitude, wonder, and even a glimmer of optimism that the world can be a better place. A tiny, dependent, and very fragile miniature person is instantly and completely 100 percent your responsibility, and the last thing you want is for anything bad to happen to him. Babies and children rely on us to meet their most basic needs: to love them, to care for them, to protect them from harm, and to heal them when they are not well.

Enter the amazing world of medical intervention marketed for babies. Thousands of scientists and doctors (and advertisers) know that you cherish your baby more than anything in the world, and they want to sell you relief from anxiety, fear, sickness, and pain. What a wonderful thing! Or is it?

The first time Miles fell off the couch onto our hardwood floor, I was of course sitting right next to him, and I felt like an awful parent, only nine months into my new "job." *Would I be fired?* I wondered.

The first time Miles split his lip, several months later, he was running with a kazoo in his mouth, under my mother-in-law's watchful eye. So of course I half-jokingly decided that she was an awful grandma! I can say this lightly now, but seeing blood in a tiny mouth for the first time really shakes some people up, and I was one of them. I wanted to take all of his pain away, but I also did not know how to do it at first.

When Miles was three and a half, he fell in a public bathroom and cracked his tooth on the porcelain toilet seat. I felt like the world had stopped spinning and that everything was moving in slow motion as my husband brought Miles's limp, sobbing body toward me. I very calmly handed four-month-old Fred to my husband and took Miles in my arms like a baby. In an even and eerily pleasant voice, I asked someone for a bottle of water, with which I washed the blood away from his teeth and gums, which enabled me to isolate the source of the blood. Then I whispered gently to him and held him as he cried. I felt a strange sense of calm come over me as I realized intuitively, for the first time, that I was the best person to take care of him at that moment and that everything he needed right then was mine to give him.

Did I always know how to care for hurting children calmly and confidently? No way. I don't even know if it emerged until my second son was born. Even now, I don't always handle things perfectly. But emerge it did, and it can for you, too.

Here is an alphabetical list of the medical issues we most commonly have dealt with in our home.

Baby acne

Bumps, bruises

Cough/croup

Cradle cap

Earache

Fever (mild to 104°)

Headache (isolated as well as sinus pressure)

Insect bites (including stinging insects)

Plantar warts (on Miles's index finger)

Plugged tear duct/eye inflammation (as distinguished from diagnosed pinkeye)

Respiratory flu (congestion, runny nose, weepy eyes, exhaustion)

Runny nose (clear)

Runny nose (thick and yellow or green)

Skinned knees, split lips, and splinters

Skin rashes (of unknown origin, heat-related or the dark-pinkish tender rash that shows up in the crevices of chubby babies' groins and armpits—fun!)

Stomach flu (vomiting, diarrhea, lethargy, achiness)

Stomachache

Teething pain and discomfort, swollen gums

Thrush

Given that impressive list of sicknesses, ailments, and "boo-boos," would it shock you if I told you that neither of our children has ever been on antibiotics or admitted to any hospital? Maybe it would surprise you that we have had only two non-checkup appointments with our pediatrician in six years, and we do all of our own medical care from the home.

I have used acetaminophen (found in Tylenol) maybe six times in six years. I have never given my children ibuprofen (found in Motrin and Advil). I have never administered any medication for teething pain, nor have I ever used antibiotic ointment (found in Neosporin), antihistamines (such as Benadryl), cough syrups, or steroids (as in cortisone creams).

Right about now you are probably thinking that I can most typically be found hovering over a pot of steaming, bubbling greenish gruel filled with eye of newt, crocodile tail, and essence of burdock root for all of our family's ailments. Well, I do *not* routinely brew up bubbling greenish gruel to fix what ails us (in a vegan house, those ingredients wouldn't fly anyway). I do not say all of this to show you how amazing I am; I am as much a nervous mother hen as the next person. I tell you all of this because tapping in to your intuition extends to healing and understanding a hurting baby, and you can save money, time, and energy by learning about helping your baby with things that are most often found in your kitchen cabinet, in your head and your heart, and in your arms.

A History of Illness

For almost all of human history, people have gotten sick and died. Babies have gotten sick and died. People have suffered from diseases that we now cure with a single pill, and otherwise healthy and strong adults have been brought to an early grave by something that can be prevented simply by washing your hands and minding who sneezes and coughs on you. That medicine can protect us, cure us, and educate us is a tremendous contribution to our quality (and length) of life. I am grateful to the men and women who risked their lives and gave their time and energy to do research and make progress in the name of science.

That being said, for all of human history, there have been useful medical tools outside of traditional medicine. Often referred to collectively as folk medicine (or, if your family was from another country, "weird stuff your grandma used to do to you"), the healing and protective powers of foods, herbs, and remedies from common elements in nature have been used for thousands of years. I do not claim that folk medicine or holistic medicine alone can cure every ill. But for the time being, let's just agree that traditional Western medicine is not the *only* thing that works to make you feel better, depending, of course, on what ails you. (I will leave to medical experts the topics of chronic childhood illnesses, resources for which can be found in abundance elsewhere.)

It may come as a surprise or perhaps even a shock to learn that many holistic people believe that sickness happens for a reason. Chinese medicine has recognized for thousands of years that sickness and ailments represent an imbalance and are an expression of something that needs fixing in your physical and emotional or spiritual makeup. Whether it be a virus (an invader that uses your body as a host), a bacteria (a living and reproducing "creature" that invades your body), or a variety of conditions that cause pain or discomfort, your body was made to heal, and babies' bodies have this ability as well.

When you have a new baby, it is incredible how quickly and intensely your panic can set in when your baby is not well. New mothers especially are hormonally primed to know instinctively when something is not right with our babies. It can't always be explained fully by the parents who experience this, but they will often report that baby just "doesn't seem right," even if the baby is only hours old. This is the result of hundreds of thousands of years of evolution working their magic right before your eyes. The hormones of vigilance and stress function in the complex midbrain to give us an understanding of our baby's nonverbal cues, body language, and overall "tone," even if she is not yet able to even sit up straight.

What you also intuitively feel, though, and what most doctors, nurses, and family and friends will tell you, is that a hurting baby should not have to hurt. Western medication makes it so that we can sleep, and rest assured that baby can sleep, too. If they are coughing, they shouldn't have to. If they are runny, they needn't be. If they are flush with fever, let's lower that fever! If they can't go potty, give them something to make them go. Imagining a coughing, runny, feverish, constipated baby is probably enough to make you run out and stock up your medicine cabinet right now. But before you do that, read on.

Are You TOO Worried About Your Baby?

Fears about a baby's well-being are normal and natural. There is ample evidence that these kinds of fears are hormonally governed—in other words, as your hormones foster attachment and the ability to nurse, they also foster behaviors and concerns that seek to protect your baby.

But some women find these fears prominent, intrusive, and sometimes very intense, especially in the first months postpartum. If you aren't sure whether what you're feeling is normal, a doctor or midwife can help assess if these feelings are within the range of what is to be expected.

Attachment Parenting and Your Hurting Baby

This seems an appropriate time to explain a significant aspect of our family's general and firm belief in using as little medical intervention for nonserious medical matters as possible. It is our conviction that pain is an indicator of something amiss; however, our job as parents is not only to make things not hurt but also to teach our children that we are organisms who are not impenetrable and immortal. Rather, we experience physical sensations that indicate a need for attention and often rest and comfort, but that there is not, nor should there be, a "pill for every ill." There are those who will claim that teaching a young child to reach into the medicine cabinet every time something hurts sets them up for addictive or chemical dependency, but I would not take it that far, nor do we need to in order to make this point.

I believe that part of parenting is seeing that a hurting child needs attention and care as well as treatment, but what often makes them feel better is being held and comforted. A hurting baby is talking to you, and what he is saying is that he needs your help. Sometimes that help comes in a bottle or a pill, and sometimes it comes from your arms.

I remember distinctly being home from school sick when I was a child. Usually it was the flu that kept me home under my mother's watchful eye, as she had the more flexible schedule of my parents (my dad was a junior high teacher and my mother worked in a half-day nursery school at our synagogue). I remember she would set me up in my bed, propped up with pillows and books and dolls, as she gave me medicine along with her favorite get-better snacks: steamed white rice, ginger ale, and chocolate (don't ask; it made me feel good, okay?). She would tuck me in for naps and when I would awake, the first thing I did was shout to her, "I'm up, Mom!" I wanted her near me. I wanted her to feel my forehead and kiss me and read to me and sit with me. I am certain that the medicine she gave me made me feel better, but I also know that it just felt good to be close to her when I was hurting.

Your baby understands this need even more acutely, although she can't shout, "I'm up, Mom!" What babies do is fuss and cry and scream and squirm. They refuse to lie docile in a bassinet or crib, and parents lament to understanding friends, "All she wants is for me to *hold* her! Doesn't she understand that I have things to do?" Well, she does and she doesn't. Hurting children know what feels good, and guess what? It's you. When they are nauseated, throwing up, feverish, and achy, rocking feels good. Holding feels good. Medications that induce sleep give parents a break, but they do not necessarily meet a baby's immediate need for you to heal her with your touch and your attention and love.

People often claim that their babies won't get better unless they rest, and so that's why they give Western medication. And it is true that medication can allow babies to rest when pain keeps them from being able to do so. But whoever decided that babies need the same amount and kind of sleep when they're ill that they do when not ill? And who set those standards? I have found that the hours I have spent walking my sick babies around has been time that I could truly tap in to what they needed even more than in their healthy hours; they spoke a different language when they were sick, and it was incumbent upon me to learn this language. Having children who started speaking quite late meant I dealt with numerous sicknesses before my children could articulate their pain. Working through sickness with them in my arms and on my lap allowed me to tap in to another level of their communication and empowered me to know that I was the best caregiver for them in all situations.

Now, I am not arguing in favor of being medically negligent by any means. Medical professionals should be sought promptly for anything that you deem important and necessary to seek attention for. In addition, children with medical conditions, histories, or allergies need to be watched with special care. However, too often I see healthy children being medicated with pain relievers, anti-inflammatories, cortisone creams, expensive bugbite lotions, antihistamines, and nasal sprays when an ice pack, rest, and even temporary dietary modifications and good old-fashioned holding would probably set them on their way in shorter course.

Three Kinds of Medical Needs

There are three categories of medical needs to understand: what our family calls "boo-boos," viruses, and bacterial infections.

"Boo-boos"

A large majority of stuff that hurts babies and kids falls under a general category that we in our house refer to as "boo-boos." This nomenclature is not intended to diminish the hurt that a child experiences, but it helps us frame the hurt so that we can best treat it. Into this category fall the following: baby acne/cradle cap, bumps, bruises, headache (isolated as well as sinus pressure), insect bites (including stinging insects), skinned knees, split lips, splinters, skin rashes (of unknown origin, heat-related, or the rash that accumulates in the crevices of the skin), stomachaches, teething pain and discomfort, swollen gums, and thrush.

We often say our child has "boo-boo arm" or "boo-boo knee" rather than saddle him with the concept of abrasion, and what we try to communicate is that sometimes things hurt and there is no medicine to make it stop hurting right away. We consciously seek out and apply *treatment*, even if we choose not to administer *medicine*. The difference between treatment and medicine is that treatment seeks to soothe a hurt, and medicine seeks to make something stop hurting. Treatments we frequently use include ice, massage, essential oils, nonmedicinal household items such as baking soda, vinegar, hydrogen peroxide, cornstarch, onion and garlic, nonmedicinal creams and lotions derived from plants, and the power of healing foods and teas.

Many holistic families use techniques such as homeopathy, craniosacral therapy, osteopathic medicine, and chiropractic care for newborns, and through childhood and adulthood. The scope of these kinds of holistic treatments has been well documented and researched, but is beyond the scope of this chapter. (See the Resources section.)

Viruses

A virus is an invader to your body that typically lives inside you, unseen. Viruses have their own ability to replicate their genetic information, but they need your body as a host to gain resources to stay alive. Once your body stops the hosting, the party's over and the virus leaves or dies. Some examples of viruses include the common cold, influenza (the flu), plantar warts, herpes (which shows itself outside of your body as a cold sore), and approximately 70 percent of ear infections. The following are usually caused by a virus: stomach and respiratory flu, all varieties of runny noses, plugged tear duct/ eye inflammation, cough/croup, earaches, and fevers.

Viruses do not go away because of medicine or treatment—the only option is letting them live out their life cycle and die. Antibiotics do not help kill viruses. Viruses can cause you to hurt, though, and people use medicine to stop or reduce the pain and discomfort associated with the expressions of a virus, such as treating a fever, a runny nose, diarrhea, or the pain of a cold sore. There is nothing wrong in principle with using medicine to treat symptoms. However, there are two main problems with conventional Western medical intervention. First, they tend to use harsh chemicals to help heal baby. And second, they treat symptoms with little regard for the *reason* the symptoms are there.

Regarding the first issue, all Western medicines—*all Western medicines*—are processed by the liver. This is true for any medicine on the shelf of your local supermarket, and it is true for adults and children alike. You can get ulcers from enough ibuprofen, and although it is rare, it is true. Every person's liver processes chemicals differently, and a baby's liver is very tiny. In addition, there are recalls all the time for products manufactured for babies, and many parents do not like to use products from an industry that frequently makes errors in labeling, dosing, and contaminating.

Regarding the second issue with Western medicine, a baby's

"problem" is indeed fixed by something that causes it to *stop*. So a fever is lowered, a runny nose is dried up, and diarrhea is encouraged to simply cease. In all of these examples, the symptom is actually trying to heal the body, and conventional medicine may be interfering with the body's mechanism for naturally purging the virus. Take fever, for example. Some viruses die quickest when your body gets so hot that they cannot reproduce successfully. That's what a fever is: your body's way of most efficiently—and intuitively—killing an invader. Lowering a fever brings a baby relief from the heat but allows the virus to live longer and persist until its life cycle runs out, which may now be longer than it ought to be. A runny nose is runny because the virus is flushed out by mucus, and only when mucus leaves the body can the virus leave. Administering antihistamines that send out hormones to dry up mucus prolongs the virus being in your body. On to diarrhea. Sure, it's immensely unpleasant to have a child with diarrhea. It's even more unpleasant to have a nonverbal baby who is potty-trained thanks to elimination communication have diarrhea in a cramped hotel room in Jerusalem but unable to tell you when he has to use the potty since he is . . . nonverbal. You get the picture. Anyway, diarrhea needs to get out of your body so that you can heal. Medications that stop diarrhea may keep the virus in longer.

You get the point: no one wants their baby to suffer the pain and discomfort associated with a nasty virus. But sometimes the medications are trying to appeal to your intuitive desire to heal, and not a deeper desire for baby to be healed.

Bacteria

Bacteria are microorganisms that like to live in our bodies. Unlike viruses, which need your body as a host, bacteria don't need you, they just like you. Millions and millions of bacteria live in our bodies all of the time, such as in the lining of our gut to help us with digestion (*Escherichia coli*, also known as E. coli) and in our vaginal canals (lactobacillus). The thing about bacteria is that they are very strong and have evolved over millions of years to resist our attempts to get rid of them. Bacteria can cause such discomforts as stomach irritation, fever, and achiness, depending on their region of attack in the body (all of which can, on their own, also be due to viruses).

Antibiotics are medications that kill bacteria, although they are not typically selective, and they tend to kill off most bacteria everywhere. Ever wondered why women tend to get yeast infections when we take antibiotics? It's because antibiotics act by upsetting the bacteria in all of your body, including your vaginal canal, thus allowing too much Candida (yeast) to thrive! Antibiotics, like all medications, are processed by the liver.

Antibiotics need to be taken in full course, as directed, for the following reason: every time you take an antibiotic, the weaker bacteria die first, leaving stronger ones feeling empowered and triumphant. Then you take another dose, and the second tier of bacteria that made it through round one die off, leaving those strong ones shaking their little bacteria fists at you in defiance. This continues for ten days until they all (statistically speaking) finally die and leave you in peace. However, if you stop at any day before day ten, you are potentially allowing the stronger ones to live on and see another day of bacteria procreation. What does that mean? It means that they pass on their superstrong resilient bacteria genes to their bacteria babies, which then breed even stronger bacteria, and so on. Sometimes parents ask doctors for antibiotics for ear infections (which are viral about 70 percent of the time) and doctors give in because they feel pressured by worried parents even though they know that the antibiotics are not useful at all. Any time antibiotics are prescribed for a nonbacterial infection, they introduce this survival struggle with what would be normal bacteria. This perpetuates a new generation of ever-resilient bacteria. It is for this reason that incorrect use and administration of antibiotics has created strains of bacteria that are resistant to some antibiotics. It is also for this reason that diseases like MRSA exist; they are, by definition, resistant to antibiotics. Scary stuff.

Sometimes antibiotics are necessary and useful, and save lives. However, certain bacterial infections, such as sinus infections, can be killed without antibiotics, and they can be resolved quickly and efficiently. The less we use antibiotics for things we do not need them for, the better. It's better for our babies' bodies, and it's better for the future of our planet. We want antibiotics to work when they are absolutely needed, and we do not want to take part in breeding bacteria that are resistant to medications.

Vaccinations

Vaccines are a very hot topic, in both holistic and conventional parenting. A complete discussion of the pros and cons of vaccines, vaccine alternative schedules, and the politics of vaccines are beyond the scope of this book, but it is worth noting that educated and intelligent people from all walks of life make all kinds of decisions to suit their lifestyles and comfort levels: to vaccinate, not to vaccinate, to handpick vaccines in single shots, to vaccinate only for diseases not easily treated, and to seek out companies that manufacture vaccines without preservatives and chemicals.

Now that you have a basic understanding of viruses and bacteria, you can understand what the recommended vaccines for the first two years of your child's life are: Vaccines for viruses include chicken pox, measles, mumps, rubella, polio, hepatitis A (hand-to-hand contact), B (transmitted by body fluids: sex, blood, IV drug use), influenza (including H1N1), rotavirus, and HPV/genital warts (human papilloma virus). Vaccines for pneumococcal diseases, pertussis, and meningitis are vaccinating against bacteria, and the tetanus and diphtheria vaccines actually seek to protect against toxins that can be released from a bacteria that has been allowed to grow.

The number of recommended vaccines has quadrupled in the past thirty years. We made an informed decision not to vaccinate our children, but this is a very personal decision that should be made only after sufficient research, which today is within reach of every parent who seeks to learn about their child's health regardless of their medical knowledge or educational status. No matter what you decide for your family, resources can be found that are simple to understand, unbiased, and straightforward. Some choices are given in the Recources section.

Tapping In to Your Intuitive Healing Abilities

Almost everything you have right now in your home and in your heart is enough to cope with most of the sicknesses and ailments your child will experience. You also already have everything you need to clean your baby and keep them clean for most of their young life without purchasing one single fancy made-for-your-baby shampoo, soap, lotion, potion, or powder (see the Resources section to try out my simple and inexpensive recipe for baby shampoo). Just as you know how to parent your baby intuitively, you also know how to care for your baby intuitively.

As a general intuitive rule of thumb with regard to your baby, *never second-guess the intuitive feeling that something is not right.* I often hear parents being urged to "go away" for a night or "go out for a date" when their baby is tiny; the notion our culture presents is that "if you don't do it now and get baby used to it" . . . then what? I always wonder. You will never go out again? Your child will rule you with an iron baby fist? No! A parent's intuition that baby may not be ready for separation often indicates that the mother-baby relationship is not ready, not that the mother needs the baby more than the baby needs the mother, as is commonly misunderstood.

In the same way, listen to your intuition, which can protect your children as they do more and more adventurous things. If your child is trying a new task that has an element of danger and you have a gut feeling that your child is not ready for it, stay close and redirect if necessary. I am not suggesting that you quash a child's desire to explore, and no one wants to be the parent who hovers over a child's every new attempt at independence. Rather, I am gently reminding you that you are your baby's best watchdog, and you know your baby better than anyone. If you sense that your baby is not ready for something, you are probably right.

If your baby is asleep in another room and you have a feeling that something is not right, *check on the baby*. If you sense that your baby is in some sort of danger, go to the baby. Present mothers and fathers alike often have an intuitive sense of their baby's status that translates to knowing his or her well-being even from afar. It's not hocus-pocus, and acting on this intuition is a good thing, not a smothering one.

Another intuitive rule of thumb is the following: take care with how you speak to a hurting child. When our children hurt, it often brings up uncomfortable feelings for us: we don't want them to suffer, but we sometimes think they are being overdramatic, or we think they should be more resilient, etc. Shushing in order to stop a child from crying, and phrases like "You're okay," "Stop crying," "Big boys/girls don't cry," and "There's nothing to cry about" send a message that getting hurt and expressing your pain makes people uncomfortable. Sure, we objectively may think or even know that they are okay, but a child who falls or gets hurt is sometimes scared and startled, and she is, in her opinion, *not* okay! Crying or wanting to be held and cuddled is appropriate for both sexes. Boys and girls alike should be encouraged to express pain and discomfort without us telling them how to feel or react; it won't make them weak or "sissies." Don't we want our children to understand and care for others? Let's start with letting them express their hurt without judgment or unnecessary redirection.

We have found that naming the event even in the midst of hysteria calms children down and lets them really understand pain and boo-boos without us overtalking it or feeling we are coddling them. For example, when our boys fall and it is clear that there has been no injury but the tears are flowing, we ask, "Hurt or surprised or both?"

Even a young child can answer and in our experience, this instantly calms him down. We also affirm feelings by saying gently, "Wow, that must have hurt!" or, better yet, letting him react first. So often, adults make a bigger deal of a fall than a child does, possibly to cover up our own fear. Gasping, shouting, "OH MY GOSH!!!" and making sudden movements toward a fallen child without letting him experience the fall can cause him to be more upset than he might have been otherwise. It's okay to observe a little bit before acting.

I was once watching a dear friend's five-year-old at the park while she ran errands. He was giggling madly one second as I pushed him way up high on a swing (yes, like a rocket ship, we decided), and the next minute his little body flew through the air like a rag doll and he landed face-first in the sand. Hard. My heart stopped as I pictured my sweet trusting friend discovering her wailing injured child in my arms, or—worse yet—at a hospital. I cared for him as I would my own child, examining his limbs, giving him water, holding him, letting him cry, and naming his feelings. Remarkably, after a few spits of sand, some sandy nose-blowing, and a little holding, he was ready to play again long before I was ready for him to! The principles I used with my own children worked for this child as well. He responded to being listened to and held, which, assuming there are no significant injuries present, is really what feels the best. And yes, that friend is still my friend. Phew!

Our House's Medical Needs, Revisited

Let's return one last time to the list of ailments we have had in our family in the past six years, with more thorough descriptions of the causes as well as the treatment we have found most useful.

Baby acne: Normal. Do nothing. Don't even use soap on baby's tender skin. Water is all they need as their tender skin adjusts to shifting from living in the amniotic fluid to living in the open air.

Cradle cap: Normal; more cosmetic annoyance than a medical problem. Caused by blockage of the glands found on baby's scalp. Almond or jojoba oil (or any oil, really) and a small baby comb can loosen the flakes, which can then be gently scraped away. It may take a few shampoos after this treatment to get the oil out of the hair completely, and the treatment may need repeating once in a while. Baby may be sensitive to foods in their diet or your breastmilk, which may be contributing to cradle cap.

Bumps, bruises: Holding and cuddling work well, as does an ice pack; we have one in the shape of a puppy dog, which makes the application as enjoyable as possible and also works as a great distraction from the fall. It's hard to get the image out of my head of a hysterical Miles running through the house after a fall, screaming at the top of his lungs: "I NEED PUPPY DOG!"

Cough/croup: Viral coughs can linger for weeks without cause for concern, especially if baby is alert, active, nursing, and eating/drinking well, and has no rattling in the chest; it's just the way some viruses take their leave—no medication necessary. Coughing can keep children awake, so we use a nonmedicinal herbal chest rub that releases soothing vapors. Croup causes a terribly disturbing barking seal-like sound emanating from your tiny child's throat. It goes away on its own, often turning into what looks like a strong cold. Salty air (take a drive along the coast or spend time near salt water if you can) is good for croup. If a baby is struggling to breathe, seek medical help immediately.

Earache: As I mentioned, about 70 percent of earaches are *not* bacterial and therefore do not require antibiotics. What they do need is rest and treatment for discomfort. We recommend garlic drops in the ears, breastmilk in the ears (!), and diluted hydrogen peroxide dosed appropriately for your baby (see the Resources section for sources that discuss appropriate dosages).

Fever: Fever can be related to a bacterial infection but is most commonly viral and can appear as an isolated event, related to cutting a tooth (even if you can't see one emerging), or along with a flu.

Fever is there to kill the virus, so first go to nonmedicinal treatments such as tepid baths (our boys never liked these), cold washcloths, minimal clothing, and close monitoring of baby's level of energy. Some people are fine with children getting very hot, but you have to decide what you are comfortable with. We discovered the excruciatingly scary way that our younger son is prone to seizures from even mild fevers. But after the first week of fevers after his first seizure, and with our pediatrician's close guidance, we have successfully managed his fevers without medication.

Headache: In my experience, headaches are usually associated with colds and flus and we use cold washcloths, lavender oil infused or rubbed on temples, and warm baths with a few drops of lavender oil to calm as well as treat the headache.

Insect bites (including stinging insects): Tea tree and lavender oils are known for their anti-inflammatory properties. Breastmilk also soothes bites and stings.

Plugged tear duct/eye inflammation (as distinguished from diagnosed pink-eye): Gentle and frequent massage of baby's tear duct (toward the bridge of the nose) and breastmilk squirted or dropped into the eye every time you nurse clears this problem up very quickly, in our experience.

Respiratory flu (congestion, runny nose, weepy eyes, exhaustion): A few drops of eucalyptus oil in the bottom of a shower basin with hot water running can steam up a bathroom and allow relief from congestion; a cut-up onion wrapped in a sack or cloth handkerchief and placed near a child's pillow encourages the mucus membranes to run (and thus gets the virus out); rest and fluids help overall healing.

Runny nose: See above.

Skinned knees, split lips, and splinters: The threes S's. Skinned knees get ice (if appropriate), kisses, and a nonmedicinal cream (we like calendula); split lips get ice—and avoid salty or acidic foods for a few days; splinters usually work themselves out, believe it or not, but tweezers used by a stuffed animal named Dr. Bear really help, with

Dr. Bear applying calendula cream while speaking in an absurdly high-pitched British accent.

Skin rashes: Airing out of simple rashes helps better than any cream, as does breastmilk applied liberally, especially to the creases of chubby babies' groins and armpits. For diaper rash, take off that diaper for even a few hours; you will be amazed what *air* can do.

Stomach flu: This is a case of waiting out the worst of it, avoiding foods too hard for the stomach to digest (like high protein foods such as meats and dairy), and encouraging foods that bind, such as BRAT: Bananas, Rice, Applesauce, and Toast. Encourage fluids, but try not to freak out if even a tablespoon of water makes your child throw up all over again. Speaking of throwing up, here's something I decided: I would never make my child throw up into the toilet. I know it makes life easier, but it's actually really gross for a kid, and I have two techniques I use instead: 1) sitting my children on my lap over the bathtub, or 2) having a small low bucket and pile of old towels handy next to where they are so that if they throw up, I can provide them a place to do it that doesn't involve me flinging their bodies all around as I rush them to the bathroom. I find it really increases their dignity and allows them to not feel like such a burden when they are throwing up. It's only laundry, and it's really not that bad, so please consider it! Know the signs of true dehydration (dry lips, weakness, unresponsiveness) and stay close to your child to monitor them. Pedialyte and similar beverages are not always needed, so don't assume your child needs them at the first sign of flu.

Stomachache: The old-fashioned hot water bottle works wonders, as do chamomile herbal tea and chamomile essential oil.

Teething pain and discomfort, swollen gums: This is a tough one. Some people swear by homeopathic remedies for teething, but we found that the best remedies were nursing, nursing, nursing, and a wooden teething ring and frozen peas (when baby is old enough to suck on them). Some kids like ice chips; ours never did. Did I mention nursing was our best and most reliable source of teething treatment?

Thrush: You do not need to give your baby prescription antifungal creams if they have thrush. Vinegar and baking soda disrupt the pH of Candida's optimal growth environment, and they can be swabbed on the inside of baby's cheeks. Probiotics are also available in a powder form (nondairy is available as well) that can be swabbed on the inside of baby's cheeks. If you are nursing, seek the support of a lactation consultant or La Leche League to learn ways to keep thrush at bay, for mama and baby.

In Conclusion

Parenting with your child's secure attachment and relationship to you for the long run in mind goes well beyond diapering, feeding a newborn, and adjusting to the lack of sleep. It implies a total and complete awareness of your children's bodily functions and needs, and it also implies understanding their bodies in sickness as well as in health. Foregoing Western medicine does not always make life easier in the short-term, and this is not an all-or-nothing enterprise. Take each sickness and ailment independently and see what works for your family. Try to remember that most things we encounter are, fortunately, not fatal, and teaching children that their bodies are both fragile and resilient is a wonderful lesson.

No one wants their child to suffer, but we also need to be careful not to raise children who reach for a pill every time life is hard, physically or emotionally. Much as I seek to protect my children from the realities of the harsh world before they are ready, their body is one arena where I want them to know exactly what they feel, to know what makes them feel better, and to know how to communicate their needs.

A few years back, when the H1N1 strain of flu arrived in Southern California and my boys were one and four, our household got hit with what was most likely H1N1. Miles, my husband, and I had it, but baby Fred was spared. Poor Miles threw up for the better part of three days, had a raging fever, and was so fatigued that he could not stand up. I spent those days glued to the couch sitting vigil with him, as if he was the newborn in the NICU that he was four years before. I was alternately covered with tears, throw-up, and sweat, and I felt both so exhausted and also so acutely aware what a blessing it is to have a healthy child. I felt in tune with parents everywhere who have had a sick child in their arms, for whatever the reason. I felt grateful that I lived in a country where medical care is available, as is clean water with which to nourish my boy, something that not every parent has at his or her fingertips.

Children hurt for a lot of different reasons, and a parent's desire for a child to be free of pain is universal. I implore you to take very seriously the charge given to you: protect this tiny dependent person not only with what Western medicine can offer you, but also with the intuition that is yours simply because you are a caring, loving, and resourceful parent.

10

Baby Doesn't Need Pressure:
Letting Kids Be Kids

Imagine your average one-year-old on a desert island with some other one-year-olds. Don't be too distraught; there's no abandonment aspect to this exercise. I'm not leaving him there forever, just for now.

I would venture to guess that the average one-year-old on a desert island would probably never think to invent a fork if he didn't have one when they arrived on the island; he would simply eat with his hands quite happily and thrive just the same, manners be darned. If you handed a desert island baby something that had fallen out of reach, he would not utter the words "Thank you," nor would he indicate in any way that he appreciated your kindness; he would take the item and continue on his merry, rude way. If on that desert island, another child had something that he wanted to play with, I guarantee you that without the slightest consideration or shame, he would go up to that child and grab it from her hands, using force if necessary to obtain and maintain the desired object. This would be even more pronounced if one child was younger or perceived to be weaker than the other.

Imagine also that this desert island has no televisions, no DVD players, no CDs, no books, no supposedly brain-stimulating Exer-Saucers (consisting of a seat for baby surrounded by dozens of stimulating bells and whistles, often with letters and numbers), no pens or pencils or crayons, and no flash cards. Without adult supervision, would a child in this environment learn to feel emotions and express them? Yes. Would he learn to read, write, perform math and, generally speaking, achieve our culture's academic milestones? Without guidance or instruction, no.

So what's my point? This desert island scenario presents us with a quandary of sorts. Without adults around, it appears that children would have no apparent concept of politeness or manners (eating with their hands rather than designing a utensil, not uttering "thank you" when someone helps them, and the like), they would seek out what they want when they wanted it with Machiavellian intensity and no apparent concern for the feelings of others nor the concept of sharing, and they would learn basic emotions but not academics.

Is this okay?

We intuitively want our children to function well socially and culturally, and this tends to mean emphasizing politeness (in varying forms), sharing (also in varying forms), and achievement in academics. That children need us to help them learn things, to guide their development, and to provide our experience in order to shape theirs is unquestionable. However, what has resulted in the culture of parenting that is considered the mainstream today is a sometimes covert and sometimes less obvious *pressure* to be polite, to share, and to excel in academics.

Now, I am sure you are thinking, "Well, who wouldn't want their child to be polite? To share? To be smart?" And I am going to answer very simply: "We all do." But the climate of pressure we have become comfortable with is, I would argue, creating a personality of obedience and incomplete understanding of the ethics and values we want our children to hold dear. We are focused so much on the outcome (a "polite" child, a "good sharer," a "supergenius") that we have lost sight of the true nature of children's desires. There are reasons children act the way that they do. Do we need to pressure them to be what we think they should be so soon in their development? Is this the only way to guarantee that your child will be the most polite, the most generous and selfless, and the kid who you can tell your friends got into an Ivy League college at sixteen? And do you even want any of that for your kid?

You guessed it: no, no, and no.

But as we have seen in other areas of parenting, when you approach manners and academic excellence from an attachment-parenting-inspired perspective, you may be surprised that there is more than one way to raise a polite and intelligent child who also shares generously.

Encouragement Versus Pressure

The distinction between encouragement and pressure is not always clear. It is certainly implicitly clear that children should be encouraged *not* to say to Great-Aunt Pearl, "You smell like rotten flowers and it makes me want to throw up." But is it necessary that we insist and enforce that young children use "please" and "thank you" all of the time? In the same vein, we want to encourage our children to demonstrate selfless generosity and play nicely together, but is there something inherently wrong about a child stating (hopefully in a gentle voice) that she doesn't want to share a toy she is enjoying with anyone who wants it? Does another child throwing a fit because she can't have a toy warrant it being given to her? What kind of lesson is that? Finally, we all know that in order for children to succeed and feel competent and fulfilled, they need to be encouraged to succeed academically and to master the appropriate designated skills for their optimal development and goals. But where did we get the notion that they have to learn their alphabet, their numbers, and even identify colors as soon as they *can*? I like to say the following: just because they *can* doesn't mean they *should*.

Every culture has different definitions of what is acceptable for lifestyle and behavior. For example, think of the differences between eating customs for babies raised to have early proficiency picking up tiny grains of rice with chopsticks versus those for Ethiopians, who traditionally eat with their fingers. Or what about the kinds of toys children play with? In the North African country of Eritrea, playing with tires, flying kites, and racing marbles are common pastimes, while children in affluent suburbs of most large cities all over the world are likely to be found playing video games on bedazzled cell phones or spending hours on Facebook on their personal laptops. Consider the differences even between people in the same country; people from the South in the United States can have very different behaviors, habits, and standards than people living in Beverly Hills, California!

Western culture highly values politeness and manners. The parenting culture of the West and much of the developed world places a high value on children "sharing" (although many adults and most political institutions could certainly learn a thing or two in this area!). In addition, accelerated learning and high standards for academic intelligence that is measurable by tests is increasingly encouraged in our culture and many others around the world.

In order for our children to develop in a healthy and organic fashion, we should examine what children *need* and *want* to do and not simply what they *can* do once the appropriate training or pressure is applied.

Politeness

I was a polite child. My parents were old-fashioned in that 1940s/1950s way, so I was the kid who called my friends' parents by "Mr." and "Mrs." I don't think I was obnoxious in an tush-kissing, obsequious, Eddie Haskell kind of way, but I recall vividly appreciating things that were done for me and trying to communicate that to my family and others as well. I also have no conscious memory of being told to be polite. I had a friend whose parents hovered over her whenever she received a gift, a ride, or a glass of water. "Say thank you." "Say please." Or the most complicated, perhaps: "Say you're sorry. *Like you mean it!*" Sometimes parents whisper these instructions a bit too loudly in a child's ear, as if no one can see that they are aggressively directing from the wings.

I was once at the park with my sons, and a three-year-old boy whom we did not know was using one of our sand toys, a small plastic block shaped like a castle. (One of my rules for our boys is that whatever we take to the park is for all the kids there to play with; if it's too special to let others play with it, leave it at home!) When it was time for this boy to go home, his mother reminded him to give back the castle, which he did by tossing it at me from a good three feet away. It landed gently at my feet and I giggled at his obedience and sweet lack of finesse that only a three-year-old can demonstrate, while inwardly noting that his mother probably didn't have that method of delivery in mind.

I was right; she looked very disappointed and said to him sternly, "Say you're sorry." He mumbled a lackluster "Sorry" as I tried to open my mouth to say, "It's okay!" She didn't think he said it loud enough, so she told him to say it again and to speak louder. This made the situation even more awkward because: 1) I had heard him the first time, and 2) I did not need an apology! If he had deliberately tried to hurt me with malicious intent, I could see having a meaningful exchange about the value of empathy, but this was not the case. This was a plastic castle being returned as she had asked, just not as politely as she desired.

Whether or not you agree with me that I did not need an apology from castle boy, I think you would agree that it is awkward and sometimes embarrassing when a child is told to be polite. Some children are so used to it that they instantly cultivate a blank stare, and the words "thank you" lose all meaning as they come tumbling out in a robotic drone. But many children squirm and look downward as they utter their politeness, probably because when you are pressured to be polite, it also can stimulate a sense of shame that you didn't come to it on your own. And shame is not fun for a child, or an adult, for that matter.

Of course we want our children to be nice, and I think a lot of people see pressuring a child to be polite as helping them navigate the world. They feel it is their job to teach a child to be polite and that consistency is the key.

But is this the only way?

I would argue no, and I am using my sons as an example. By using two children as my data set, I do a great disservice to the fine university that awarded me my PhD, but for the sake of argument, just go with me on this. We never told our sons to say "please," "thank you," or "I'm sorry." And they are very polite children.

So it's not a simple equation: make them be polite + opportunities to be polite = polite. We have found that true, instinctive, and authentic politeness comes from watching adults relate politely, having open conversations about what behavior makes people feel good and what kinds of actions and words hurt others, and observing with your child the reactions that occur when people are mistreated. When our sons get presents from friends or even family, they are still learning to spontaneously generate a "thank you." So we model it, by sharing in our child's excitement and thanking the giver of the gift so that our sons can hear it. They don't have to mimic us, but with time, we have found that they do. Teaching manners without pressure is a wonderful opportunity to explore the reasons behind politeness rather than just the mechanics of it.

When our older son was about four, he received a gift he was not thrilled about from my parents (he was apparently hoping for a larger gift than he actually received). He had trouble hiding his disappointment, but I didn't embarrass him about it. I thanked my parents, and when we were alone, I explained to Miles that sometimes people miss the mark or get us something we are not happy about, but there is value in their wanting to be kind with a present, and we can thank them for their intent, even if we don't like the gift. He looked grumpy, and I think my parents must have been thinking, *That child needs to learn some manners!* But with time, he is learning more, and I am learning to let my parents' feelings about my methods in this area be *their* feelings.

It has also helped to speak to our parents when the kids are not around about our expectations of these small people. Although they may not agree, it helps for them to hear that my husband and I have given a lot of thought to how we want our children to be taught to experience their feelings and that we desire what they would probably call "good behavior." We acknowledge that being polite and appreciative are values that we cherish just as they do and that we hope we will all see the day soon when these beloved children prove that gentle encouragement and modeling work. You get more bees with honey, so in general, give credence to your elders and their notions of what is okay, and it will buy you a lot of leeway as your children develop at their own pace.

In my experience, modeling politeness and decency while communicating about human interaction in the process beat pressure, possible shame, and robotic drones any day.

Sharing

I may lose some of you when I tell you this next thing about me: I hate for kids to share. Actually, that's not entirely true. I hate *forcing* kids to share. When people hear this, they usually stare at me incredulously. They must be thinking: *Are you even invited to anyone's house for playdates? What kind of child do you expect to raise? What possible harm is there in teaching the wonderful value of sharing, which makes the world a nice place to live in? Your kids must be miserable playmates and tyrants who rule you and their surroundings based on their greed, selfishness, and self-centeredness!* Okay, that last one is a bit harsh, but I know someone has thought it, so it deserves to be voiced.

Well, I promise you that none of this is the case. My children do share, and they often share more regularly and with more joy than some children they play with who were raised being pressured to share. In addition, my boys often *initiate* sharing. How? We have found that children learn to share when they are ready, and they don't need us to tell them to share, because, as with politeness, we can simply show them how.

Most people think of sharing as a skill you teach your child, much like tying a shoe or using a fork. We are told that with enough repetition and reinforcement, sharing becomes second nature. Sharing is caring, the saying goes. Right?

When you think about it, sharing is a complicated and fairly sophisticated concept. It involves you wanting something and reducing or postponing your desire for it for the altruistic reason that someone else wants it. Do we do this as adults? Not as often as we would like to believe. For example, if I want your purse, do you have to share it with me? If I find your husband fascinating, attractive, and witty, do I get to share him with you? No and no. In my marriage, if I want some of my husband's french fries, he has made it clear that even that is a source of negotiation.

As adults, we know that sometimes things are for sharing and sometimes they are not for sharing. We get to choose and decide on a case-by-case basis. So why are children different? A normal stage of development, from about six months until well into the second year, is asserting your place in the world, testing limits, and exploring people's reactions to your actions. The concept of voluntarily sharing emerges when a child has been allowed to develop and exercise autonomy, self-discipline, and empathy.

Perhaps you are thinking that your children will not follow your lead unless you pressure them to. Perhaps you are thinking that no child would ever do anything generous unless pressured to. Do you wonder how you would deal with the interactions and disputes that arise when sharing is *not* forced? Does the thought of letting your kid cling to a prized baby doll, miniature soccer ball, silver marble, or piece of lint terrify you? I can tell you I have handled the lint incident and all of the others as well, and it can be done without anyone needing a sedative. Let's look at a few common things that can happen when you back off on pressuring kids to share.

Hurt feelings

As adults, many of us find other people's hurt feelings very uncomfortable to sit with. You probably know people like this: the second they see that someone is grumpy and unhappy with their choice of restaurant or radio station, they apologize and quickly change their mind to match the grump's. Sometimes people do this in a spirit of camaraderie and friendly compromise, but oftentimes people do it because they cannot tolerate the hurt feelings that result from a difference of opinion.

Children raised by such parents are often told preemptively to share, and when another child wants something that they have, you will see the parent step in and whisper gently (or forcefully through gritted teeth), "He really wants that. You *have to* share."

Now, this doesn't really make logical sense if you think about it. A child intuitively knows when he wants something. Why should another child wanting it at the same moment in time trump their desires?

The way we handle situations like this are the following. If my child is the one with the desired object and another child wants it and begins crying or even screaming for it, I will make an observation out loud: "I see that so-and-so really wants that toy." I let that sit. I watch my child watch the other child. "I see he is very upset." And I let that sit. And I watch my child watch. At first, my child may shrug and keep playing, and I get to show empathy to the other child, even though it's really hard for me to see a child upset, and I almost always want to cave in and say, "Share!" I will offer (loud enough for both children to hear), "Miles is having a turn right now. It will be your turn when he is done."

Between you and me, "when he is done" in actuality may not come before we leave the park or the house where the episode is occurring. My kid may play with that thing until sundown and you may not get a turn. Sorry, but it's true. But it is also true that when Miles is done with it, he will no longer be using it and someone else can. In this way, "Share!" is transformed into a concept: people take turns with things and we have empathy when someone's feelings are hurt or when she is disappointed. But that doesn't mean that every time this occurs, we have to fix everyone's hurt feelings at the expense of ours.

Eventually, we found that both of our boys, around the age of two, upon seeing an upset child, initiated finishing their play so that they could give a friend a turn with an item. They didn't do this out of fear or a feeling that they didn't deserve it; they simply saw that someone wanted a turn and, more times than not, helped make that happen with care and gentleness. We have found that letting children see what hurt and disappointment looks like allows them to understand these emotions more deeply and then act appropriately. You don't need to pressure children to share; let them cultivate empathy, sensitivity, and generosity, and let them amaze you.

Physical struggles and kid-on-kid violence

What often happens when children want each other's things is that they become physical, especially if they are preverbal or are still mastering language. This can look like anything from tugging at the object to pushing, hitting, and outright violence of many flavors, depending on the personalities involved. Now, sometimes children may need to be separated from each other if there is bodily harm imminent. Many times children choose to be physical as a way to communicate the intensity of their intentions, and harm does not result. I have seen many a skilled teacher and parent stay close to children who are being physical *without* separating them and pressuring them to "Cut it out!" and "Just share!" in order to end the dispute. Repeating the suggestions above often gives children the space and focus to decide how to proceed, be it by sharing or not sharing. Physical violence is never an okay way to communicate, but caution should be taken about intervening too early lest they see conflict as something to avoid rather than work through together.

Parents who don't agree with you

One of the most difficult situations I have encountered surrounding the issue of sharing is parents who are not on board. This can look like one of two things: 1) My child wants something and the parent of the child who has it forces his or her child to share, or 2) Another child wants something my child has and his or her parent wants my child to share it.

In the first case, I make sure not to interfere with the parent and child, but I find a convenient way very early in the discussion is to say to the parent something like "I understand that sharing may be important for you and I don't want to step on your toes, but it is okay with me if your child doesn't want to share that right now."

Often the parent thinks I am "just being nice," but I reiterate and rephrase it as needed to communicate that if it is a lesson they are working on, that's great, but please do not encourage sharing because of my child's hurt feelings or protestations. I find that this not only communicates my stance to the other party, it also allows my child to hear my reasoning without my directly lecturing them about it.

The second case of my kid not sharing and a parent wanting him to, is trickier—and these kinds of situations often leave me wondering why I even bothered to go to the park at all if I was not up for this flavor of interaction. In general, I don't like parents who pressure my child about pretty much anything; if anything needs to be dealt with regarding their not liking my kid's behavior, I prefer they talk to me, unless my child is causing someone to be in immediate physical or psychological danger. Children are not adults, and adults should talk to adults. Parents can help facilitate discussions between children, but any adult other than a child's parent is perceived by kids as an authority figure, and that can color the interactions unfairly.

So, back to the sticky situation. If a parent asks my child to share, I step in and help my child understand what is going on. I state to my child the same things that I discussed above regarding another child's "uncomfortable feelings," and I speak to the other child about it with my child, rather than get into a parent-parent fight about who deserves the toy. My general rule is that if I want to operate in public arenas where there are people who do not agree with my style of parenting or sharing, I may need to use a little assuaging. I may suggest a different toy to my child or to the other child, suggest working on something together (such as making train tracks instead of fighting over who holds which train car). Or I may offer other alternatives to pressuring my child to share, such as taking out a new object for the other child—and hoping my child doesn't decide to want *that one* instead.

Sometimes parents will get annoyed with me and walk away and I have to be okay with that. More often than not, children surprise us by finding creative ways to handle their desires, their emotions, and their concepts of what is "right." What results when they have the room to grow empathy naturally is a stronger and longer-lasting compassion, which can serve as a lesson for some of us adults about conflict resolution.

Achievement and Excellence

Whereas the notion of pressuring small children to be polite or to share has some degree of variability from family to family, the issue of encouragement to achieve academic excellence or to start learning early on is a bit more complicated. Most people would never claim that they are pressuring their children to learn; rather, they are "encouraging" them, "fostering in them" a love for learning/reading/math/concert violin, "opening their minds," and giving their child "the best possible start" on a path of success that, in our culture, is determined by and large by how "smart" you are. Putting aside the concept of "pressure" for the moment, what could possibly be wrong with encouraging learning at the earliest possible age for your child?

Think about what life would be like without preschool. Imagine if it didn't exist. Imagine that children did not start school until kindergarten, which would be at about five or six years old. Assuming you did not use day care for the years preceding the start of kindergarten, what would you do with your child? With no facility to take them to and no institutionalized guidance for what they "should" be learning, what would your days look like? Well, up until forty years ago, there was no such thing as preschool. That's right, you heard me: *no preschool!* The "greatest generation" of Americans had no formal schooling until they were five or six years old. Approximately 70 percent of women in 1970 stayed home with their children full-time (as opposed to about 20 percent in 2009), and preschool became popular only as the women's liberation movement gained popularity and women increasingly sought employment outside of the home.

What was life like for a child without preschool before this shift in labor and child-care demands? Children played, they spent time with Mom on chores, and they visited with friends and family. Most families did not have cable television until the 1980s, so there were not thousands of channels to choose from, and you couldn't TiVO something to let your kid watch "later," because that didn't exist either. Plus, there were no DVDs or videotapes to pop in when Mom needed a break, nor were there baby-geared CDs of music designed to help your child "learn" as you drove them to and from the park.

This was not ideal for a lot of moms, but if we focus for a moment just on the child growing up in this environment, we see that children can and do learn and develop just fine without structured education when they are tiny; there have been no statistically supported scientific studies showing that children who grew up pre-1970 are any less intelligent, less developed, or less well adjusted than children growing up today. In fact, they may have a lot of skills that children today don't have, simply due to the differences in technology. (Think about patience: the average child in 1940 had no concept of computers taking too long to load, cell phones not charging fast enough, or traveling halfway around the world taking less than a week. I wonder if patience is a skill that this next generation of little ones will have a harder time developing!)

Just as we intuitively know how to parent, your child intuitively knows how to grow and develop in their early years, and this is all part of learning. Remember the image we had of one of our mammal cousins when we thought about birth? We can extend it to learning. Here are some of the intuitive ways your child learns.

We are family

If we adjust a mammal's age to that of a human developmentally, we see that a mammal learns everything they need from their mother and community in the first stage of life. This means that the most important learning is done by interacting with parents, siblings, and extended family and friends. Babies love being held and looking at people. Many baby products for sale today feature ways to get your baby to be happy *not* being held by you and looked at by you. Think of the mobiles, floor mats with dangly critters overhead, and elaborate strollers with toys attached to the handlebars. Simply being with people is the most natural thing for a human primate to do, and it teaches social standards, cooperation, appropriate expectations, and perhaps the greatest lessons of all: love and affection. Children need to learn first in our arms so that they can then learn outside of our embrace and, eventually, without it.

No comparison

Kids rarely compare themselves to others as a motivation to learn or do more. That's something adults do for them. Comparing children is something I honestly did not know existed this intensely until I had my first son. Comparing who is bigger, who is thinner, who rolls over first, who crawls and walks first, who speaks their first word and first sentence first—I even heard two mothers of newborns comparing who had the faster milk-ejection reflex! With the increasing interest in early achievement, this conversation has expanded to include who knows their colors first, who recites their ABCs first, who can count to ten first, and so on. Although it is normal for children to learn about their abilities based on (and sometimes motivated by) other children's achievements, the kind of comparing that parents do can be disturbing and divisive. Comparing sets up unrealistic concepts of how we interact, and it introduces in children the notion that they are identified by who they are taller, skinnier, or smarter than. I implore people (especially in social situations like parks and malls) to find things to talk about besides who is _____-er. Talk about your child's assets and areas they need to work on, but try to eliminate thinking of your child as a measuring stick, and they will not feel as if they always have to measure up.

This seems to be a good time for me to mention that every child develops differently and at her own pace. But what can we say about children who are not "on the bell curve" when it comes to excelling in achievement? The parents of late bloomers or "atypically developing" children are required to defend their parenting styles and choices more often than the average parent. I speak from personal experience as the mother of two boys who both sat, babbled, crawled, talked, and walked much later than their peers and than most of the "norms" you read about in parenting magazines and books. Both of my sons did not roll over or crawl when they were "supposed to," and they did not walk until seventeen months (although by then they were signing for potty and wore underwear, but who's comparing?). Both of my sons did not talk at the level "expected" for their age until well after three years old, with my younger son having as many words at two as many children have by one.

With my first son, I became very sensitive to the judgments and the ideas others had about children who don't fit the "normal" curve. I will not deny that having a child who could not roll over long after children six months younger than him could and having a child who needed me to translate broken phrases to waiters years after other kids were ordering full meals on their own was (and is) sometimes frustrating. I am ashamed to admit that I sometimes found this embarrassing. *Why can't my kids just hurry up and be like every other kid?* I sometimes think. The experience forced me to do a lot of soul-searching. What did I want from my child? What were my sons trying to tell me with their apparent patience and happiness with themselves exactly the way they were?

Most other parents would have sent their children to a speech, physical, and occupational therapist. But I had the following things that kept me from despairing over my "late-blooming" boys: 1) a mother-in-law with an excellent memory that my sons were developmentally exactly what my husband was like as a child, 2) a husband with apparently the same memories somewhere in his brain (hence his intuitive sense that our sons were totally fine), and 3) a supportive pediatrician who assured us that all was well.

Without these, I would have not only been very nervous that something was wrong, I also would have spent a tremendous amount of time, money, and energy trying to "force" development that came in its own time. Good pediatricians can usually do basic assessments in their offices, and it has become a sort of bizarre trend to have children assessed and diagnosed for a variety of delays that in many cases resolve on their own.

Respecting your children's development without comparing them to others gives your children the room to grow at their own pace, honors their specialness, and affirms your intuition. As someone who parents differently than a lot of people I know, I have been accused of stunting my children's development, encouraging clinginess by holding them "too much," and (my personal favorite) cheating them out of the ability to speak by correctly interpreting their nonverbal cues. Some people truly believe that the way they are parenting is the only right way, and this rears its head in no stronger way than when they compare their kids to mine. It's only with my second child that I have learned to pretty much ignore these ridiculous and hurtful accusations, and to pray that when those people become grandparents, they will have sweet, mellow grandchildren who develop comparatively late but are clearly fine and are simply taking their time developing.

I now know to have compassion for people who think all children can be categorized and filed as if they are in a "library of normalcy" that I finally realize does not even exist. The lessons I have learned by watching my late bloomers—patience, faith, compassion—are invaluable, and I can see that just as adults have different learning curves for new skills and challenges, children do, too.

Play

My husband and I made a personal choice not to introduce academics in any form to our children in their first five or so years of life. This included no ABC books, no singing the alphabet song, no puzzles with letters or numbers, and we even went so far as to not "teach" colors, to the dismay of my parents and in-laws ("What harm could there be in teaching him colors?!"). What we did was a lot of learning about maps and nature and the human body when our older son was around five, but none of our learning ever involved memorization or being taught by rote or even "sneaking in" learning by, for example, having letters be the focus of art activities. It's not that I don't believe in learning; on the contrary, my husband and I both pursued advanced degrees and we love education, school, and academia. We simply want to foster it in the healthiest way we see fit for our kids. There's a time and a place for everything. We of course own those classic wooden blocks with letters; we just choose not to make the letters the focal point of the blocks just yet. So how do kids learn?

Believe it or not, for the first several years of a child's life, one of the best things they can do to learn and become both intelligent and creative is to play. Not to do flash cards or "read," but just to play. Playing with blocks, pots and pans, and water and sand are some of the best things for a baby's mind. The learning, sequencing, and cause and effect that these things demonstrate speak for themselves.

Many people think that the "new" ways to teach are always better than the old ways. Meaning, if you can have electronic blocks that speak to your child in Spanish, French, and English, your children will not only be playing with blocks, they will be learning, too! Not so much. They don't always need multiple modalities in order to learn. And at the age when block play is most enticing, that's about all they should have to do at one time. Cultivating your child's love for simple toys (see chapter 8 on stuff) is a gift not only to your wallet, but also to your anxiety. It's okay for a baby or a child to simply play. They learn all the while.

Media

As babies get older and become talking, reasoning toddlers and young children, the value of imaginative play is incomparable. Schooling philosophies such as the Steiner-designed Waldorf method of education, while not perfect, have elevated the concept of imaginative play to a new level by encouraging parents to limit their child's exposure to media and emphasizing storytelling, handcrafts, and imaginative play rather than academics in the first years of a child's development. This kind of environment is a practical blueprint for what true unadulterated play looks like.

As a home that does not provide television, movies, or computer games to our boys, we have seen that when play is not based on previously viewed themed scripts or episodes of a television show, a child is truly encouraged to invent his own scenario of play. What results is not that our children sit around staring at the ceiling, nor do they run out of things to play with or about. They can play for hours, acting out activities about things that they love, be it fire stations, outer space, or many of the stories and books we read to them that don't always include pictures, thus allowing our kids to make up whatever they want to about characters and scenery. The play that non-media-exposed children come up with is not superior to the play of children who watch television or movies; it simply demonstrates that children can and do play beautifully and creatively even if they don't utilize the media outlets or the products that marketing sells us in conjunction with those outlets.

The media has adopted the cause of educating your child in fun ways, with advertisers, writers, and producers of television and movies gearing their products for children under the guise of promoting academic excellence. This makes our desires for our children to learn hard to disentangle from the barrage of products and books showing us how to make them learn. Television programs are considered okay because "they're educational!" Books are no longer just for fun; they teach the alphabet and numbers on every page. It has become increasingly difficult to find books that do *not* "teach" your child something. There are radio advertisements encouraging you to purchase a reading program designed for six-month babies, since this is the "optimal" time for them to learn—who said anything about a baby needing to learn to read?!

The issue of media is extremely complicated, and our family chooses not to have our children watch television or movies until they are much older. However, I am aware that for a lot of families, television and videos are a way to give parents a break in the morning, during the day, or at night. I think that people feel better about sticking children in front of a TV set if the program is "educational," but I would argue that if you intuitively feel weird about your child zoning out, seeming excessively fixated or distracted, or bothering you and having tantrums over wanting more TV time, then I would say using the television may not be the best thing for you or them, educational or not.

Peer Pressure

This might all sound fine and good for someone else. Someone with more time, more resources, and more patience. Someone whose kid is not like yours, because you think that your kid needs a lot of stimulation/encouragement/help. Pressure to achieve and reach either cultural or academic milestones is thoroughly ingrained in our culture, and resisting the trends of most parents in our culture is challenging and frustrating.

Trust yourself. Trust your child. Trust your intuition. Don't give in to peer pressure. There is no contest to win, no gold seal you get from the universe when your kid is the "best." Reduce the conflict with your children when they are behaving appropriately, and learn from their intensity, their desires, and their specialness.

Backing off on pressure frees you to observe more, interrupt less, and see the true nature of your child and everyone else's, too. I hate to burst your pressurized bubble, but you should honestly consider that the polite child who says "please" and "thank you" and "shares" when you tear her toy out of her hand and give it to her whiny little friend probably won't do those things when you aren't standing there making her. Imagine that by releasing the pressure and focusing instead on teaching the values and rewards of manners that you are creating a small person with a conscience, a strong sense of self, and faith in her needs rather than a robot or academic overachiever who only wants to make you stop pressuring her.

Feels good to release the pressure on yourself, too, doesn't it?

11

Baby Doesn't Need Punishment: Understanding Gentle Discipline

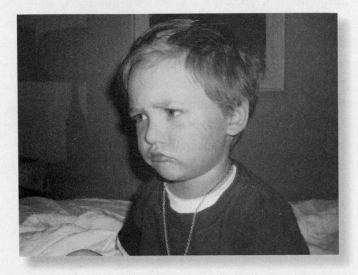

"When I was about twenty years old, I met an old pastor's wife who told me that when she was young and had her first child, she didn't believe in striking children, although spanking kids with a switch [branch] pulled from a tree was standard punishment at the time. But one day when her son was four or five, he did something that she felt warranted a spanking—the first of his life. And she told him that he would have to go outside and find a switch for her to hit him with. The boy was gone a long time. And when he came back in, he was crying. He said to her, "Mama, I couldn't find a switch, but here's a rock that you can throw at me."

—Astrid Lindgren, author, *Pippi Longstocking*

If I had a penny for every time someone explained to me why the style of discipline we use, gentle discipline, wouldn't work for them, I'd be very very rich and I'd no longer have stained carpets (which have not been replaced because my husband says it's not a financial priority). I've heard it all: "Gentle discipline only works for_____." Fill in the blank: small families, at-home moms, mellow kids, chubby babies, boys with blond hair and blue eyes who are late talkers, inhumanly superpatient moms who must possess alien DNA . . . you name it. How to discipline is one of the hottest topics in parenting, and examining your choices and considering shifting your concept of how to discipline—and how not to—is very daunting.

Many of us parent the way we were parented, even if we were not so keen on how we were parented. It's natural, and we tend to gravitate toward what is familiar, even if we start out as new parents with the best intentions to not repeat our parents' mistakes. When it comes to discipline, I know that a lot of parents start out wanting to be gentler, less violent, and less authoritarian than their parents were. But there is something about what happens during the first years of your child's life that convinces you that even Mother Teresa and Gandhi would turn to corporal punishment (or run off to Siberia) as the only reasonable way to cope with an impertinent toddler. And so you build up a set of defenses against anyone who questions that you are too harsh, too aggressive, too authoritarian, too intense.

Discussions of discipline styles invariably make people uncomfortable, and sometimes people feel guilty or ashamed when their style comes under attack. Others may become defensive, even if they secretly wish they could do things differently. Guilt, shame, and being on the defensive often lead people to feel hopeless, which in turn closes them off to the possibility of changing.

I want to say three things regarding the feelings that this discourse may bring up.

1. I am not trying to guilt or shame anyone.
2. If you do feel guilt or shame, this *may* be a message from within you that something you have been doing and believing in doesn't feel right anymore, and that is okay.
3. It is never—*never*—too late to change how you parent, especially if you desire to use a gentler form of discipline.

Children are remarkably resilient, and using less aggressive methods of discipline does not automatically doom you (or them) to unruly, boundary-less chaos. Go easy on yourself and keep reading.

Typical parenting books might start this kind of chapter describing what harsh discipline looks like, by citing examples, providing statistics showing that harsh discipline hurts your kids, and ending with how you can be the best parent in the world if only you apply the principles of gentle discipline. Well, you probably have already figured out that this is not a typical parenting book, and this will not be a typical chapter on discipline.

What I am going to do is tell you what gentle discipline is, and I will discuss how harsh discipline works against your intuition both for your child and for you, complete with examples of specific techniques that we are told work but, in reality, don't. I will explain what we have discovered works best for our family about gentle discipline, and then I will let you in on some of our family's favorite discipline tools that frame the boundaries of our interactions and create an environment where even if no one is behaving their best, we still find a way to resolve things together, with everyone's sanity and dignity mostly intact.

In consideration to my parents and my family of origin, I will refrain from discussing the details of the discipline used in my home as a child. No one who knows my family would doubt that my parents love me very much, and they did the best they could with the knowledge and resources they had. I can say the same for any and all of us. I say this not to arouse suspicion about my childhood, but rather to inform you that I was not raised in a household that exclusively used the concepts of gentle discipline as a rule, nor did they come easily to me as a parent. I have learned slowly and painfully, and I have come to believe children grow and thrive with gentle discipline.

Entire books have been written that explain from A to Z how to use gentle discipline in every imaginable scenario you can encounter (see this chapter's recommended reading in the Resources section). I won't repeat in this one chapter what it takes entire books to convey, but I want to give you some of the boiled-down, big-picture tools of gentle discipline that have resonated best with our family, from birth until now.

What Is Gentle Discipline?

Gentle discipline is a general term that, in brief, means parenting without violence, relying instead on respectful communication and seeking to see your child not as someone lesser or weaker than you who you can and should control, but rather as a partner in your life and a source of potential joy and loving interaction. Some general goals of gentle discipline include making our children feel safe with us, feeling that they are partners in their relationship with us, and finding ways for children to make better choices in behavior as opposed to simply teaching them to stop a behavior that we deem inappropriate. In addition, by nurturing respect and empathy, we teach self-discipline and encourage children to be the best that they can be.

A common misperception about gentle discipline is that it encourages and allows children to do whatever they want; that they will rule the house and become spoiled and dictatorial tyrants who hold us hostage with their every whim. This is *not* what gentle discipline is all about. Gentle discipline is *not* permissive parenting, which implies that parent and child are peers. Rather, gentle discipline is an umbrella term that describes a cooperative method of relating with and communicating your needs to your child while respecting his needs at the same time.

Gentle discipline can be used to achieve whatever structure you seek to establish in your home. Most families who practice gentle discipline still require children to be polite, considerate, and responsible—and some gentle-discipline families may appear to have more rules and expectations than families who use harsher styles of discipline! The difference is the way parents and children relate, the way language is used, and the way relationships are built up so that when children grow into adults themselves, they connect with their parents in loving and healthy ways, based on the foundations of gentle discipline that were established when they were young.

What Doesn't Work for Our Children

Sometimes it's easier to realize first what doesn't work before we can formulate what does work. Illogical consequences for undesirable behavior, name-calling or labeling your child, using your authority to arbitrarily dole out discipline, and discouraging the expression of a child's normal emotions are all examples of discipline that I see as counterintuitive to the concept of attachment parenting as I understand it.

Illogical consequences

One of the discipline techniques I see most often is giving illogical or unrelated consequences for actions that a parent seeks to stop. Common examples include these types of conditional threats: "If you don't listen to me, you can't watch TV tonight." "If you don't stop throwing your toys on the floor, you won't get dessert." "If you keep hitting your brother, I'm not going to take you to the park." Children will often stop the offending behavior when threatened with removal of privileges, sweets, or fun outings. Wouldn't you do the same? I have found that one aspect of gentle discipline that I value is that I want to have my discipline *make sense* to my children. Illogical consequences may achieve the desired outcome, but they also establish a climate of arbitrary authority and threat that I don't think works to build better relationships between us and our children. Again, it may improve behavior, but it doesn't improve relationships.

For almost every action we seek to modify, we have found logical consequences that we can use within the boundaries of gentle discipline. For example, we may say things to an older child such as "If you are not able to listen to me now, I worry that when we go out to the park today, you won't be able to listen there, either. Listening is important so that we stay safe and can communicate well at the park." Or "Balls are for throwing; books are not for throwing. If you continue to throw those books, I am going to put them away until later so that they don't get damaged." This may seem like a lot of words, and at first it may seem forced. With practice, speaking, thinking, and interacting this way become second nature.

For some actions it is hard to find a logical consequence. For example, what is the logical consequence if your child is whining? Telling her you won't ever listen to her again? What is the logical consequence of hitting? Telling him he can't use his hands the rest of the day? What we have found is that the application of gentle discipline lightens the load of stress on a family, and you may be amazed to start to see an overall decrease in otherwise prominent troublesome behaviors, thus decreasing your need for creativity in this arena. In our family, whining disappears within minutes when we gently use such phrases as "I can't hear you when you use that voice," or my personal favorite, suggested by my La Leche leader: "The answer to that voice is 'no.'" When a child throws a spoon, we say, "Spoons are for eating" and in this same vein, "Hands are for playing/eating/hugging, not hitting" makes sense to even a small person. To deal with hitting more specifically, "Hitting hurts" and "In our family we don't hit" have both worked very well as a starting point for larger discussions about how we behave with our hands and our feelings.

You have to find what works best for your family and your child. However, I implore you to use the same logic with your children that you would use with a boss, coworker, friend, or your spouse. Children are not stupid, and they feel valued when we treat them with respect. Resorting to illogical consequences serves to establish us as mighty and them as subservient; it doesn't show respect.

Name-calling/labeling

If you were ever called names by kids in school, you know that it doesn't feel good. I remember to this day the kids in my schools who were tormented for both physical differences and psychological quirks from kindergarten through high school, where shyness, being overweight, or having acne were a cause for surprisingly vicious name-calling. In elementary school, I was "shorty," "flat-chested," and "toilet water" (by some astute kids who remembered from Hebrew school that my name meant "water"). By high school, "Blossom" was enough of a name-calling to make me pretty self-conscious and introverted!

Now imagine a small child being assigned a derogatory name or label by his or her own parent. That hurts a lot, and it can stay with you much more than a name from elementary school would. I hear parents label their children as bad, bratty, spoiled, lazy, flirtatious, neurotic—you get the idea. Children hold on to the things we tell them, and it affects their self-image when we label them. Sure, sometimes kids act in ways that we don't like, but try being descriptive about a behavior rather than throwing a label on it. "I see that you are sitting on the couch when I asked you to clean up your toys from the floor. I would like you to get up and clean up your toys, please" works much better than "You're lazy!" "I see that you really want another cookie, but I said we would have one and only one" is gentler than "Don't be such a spoiled brat!" "Prickly words hurt" and "The prickly words you are using are for grown-ups" are much more sensible than "Only bad boys curse!" Watch how you talk about your children when they are not present as well; the more we speak about them to others as labels, the more we will think of them as that label.

"Because I said so"

There are many times when parenting is exhausting and overwhelming, and gentle discipline seems like way too much work. We all have these moments, and I have found that they pass eventually, and the more benefits I find in this style of parenting the quicker they pass. Even so, there are still those moments when my sweet little one asks me for the one hundredth time, "Why not?" or "Why can't I?" and I honestly feel that the best possible answer would be for me to say in a rather loud and not-so-nice voice, "BECAUSE I SAID SO!!!" Now, a rather loud and not-so-nice voice does get a child's attention, but it's attention of the wrong kind. And most children will make it very clear that an answer like that doesn't really make sense to them.

"Because I said so" types of explanations treat the child like a subject who does not deserve or warrant an explanation from us about the limits we seek to set. We won't always know answers to our children's questions, but I am sure from personal experience that "Because I said so" and "Because I'm the mama" do not do the trick.

"Don't cry"

Crying is a natural and developmentally appropriate reaction to a variety of occurrences in a child's life: fear, sadness, surprise, anxiety, hurt, and anger are the ones that come to mind when I remember why I cried as a child. Crying coming from our children can make us very uncomfortable as parents—perhaps because we oftentimes can't make the hurt go away, or because we don't want them to disturb people who may be around, or because we simply don't think that they should be crying. Whatever our motivation, children cry because they need to.

Tears have been found to contain small amounts of cortisol, the body's stress hormone. Crying may serve to release tension and stress from tiny bodies, and it is normal and healthy. Seeing crying as a natural and reasonable form of communication removes the stigma our culture associates with it. It may not be the most effective communication tool, but it is sometimes the only one small children have in their limited arsenal.

Our boys cried a lot when they fell, when their feelings were hurt, and when they were scared of new situations. (Miles cried when he saw wheelchairs for some unknown reason, and Fred still cries when he sees clowns.) Some family and friends found it funny (or perhaps uncomfortable or unsettling?) and mocked our boys' crying, albeit playfully. This is, frankly, not at all helpful, and it perpetuates the idea that children shouldn't cry when *we* think they shouldn't. If you are personally annoyed by your child "pretending" to cry, that's a different issue altogether, and even then I would argue to try to get to the root of the need for "crocodile tears." But when children cry, it's important to let them cry while helping them understand their feelings and searching for ways to help them feel better.

And as for the classic, "I'll give you something to cry about," I am pretty sure you know what I will say about that: don't say it! When children are in distress, threats used as a way to force them to stop crying can create some awfully strange and scary associations for them not just about crying but about expressing any emotion that other people don't like. And I am sure we would all agree that we want our children to grow into adults who can confidently say such things as "No thanks, I don't smoke/drink/do drugs," "Stop touching me," and "That doesn't feel good." It all starts here.

What Works for the Wrong Reasons

Now that we have examined what doesn't work, let's look at the discipline tools that seem to work—but, in fact, work for the wrong reasons. When these techniques are used, children remarkably cease "bad" behaviors, behave in an apologetic fashion, and oftentimes do not repeat the offending behavior; if they do, maybe it is not repeated as aggressively or as frequently, and eventually, we are told, the child's desire to act out the behavior is gone. In addition, many people who use these techniques point to their obedient, quiet, and well-behaved children as the proof that this is the way to go. This assumes, of course, that these wise individuals have a time machine that allows them to go back in time, raise their child without these techniques, see how the child grew up—then compare and contrast. Once the time machine finished its magic experiment, it was clear that gentle discipline did not work at all but that these harsher techniques did! Boy, are those parents lucky that they have that time machine!

Let's examine these examples of things that work, but for all the wrong reasons.

Time-outs

I know that a lot of people really like time-outs, and time-out's close cousin, the "countdown" (when a child is behaving in a way you don't want, you count backward from three, and if the behavior has not stopped by one, the child gets a time-out). There are books and manuals and equations used to calculate exactly how much time your child should be placed in a time-out, under what circumstances, and how to keep them in time-out. The idea is that when a child behaves inappropriately, he is separated from an activity/group/situation and forced (strongly encouraged?) to be alone until he can either calm down or apologize and rejoin the activity/group/situation, agreeing not to do the thing that got him removed in the first place.

You have seen time-outs if you live in any region of this country where busy parents read lots of parenting books and take their children to see pediatricians whose waiting rooms look nicer than most preschools across the country. I can often identify a child who is having a time-out first by the sound of screaming. When I identify the locus of the screaming, I typically have observed a child in a chair in the corner of a restaurant or at the park or in a car seat, alone and sobbing and usually facing a wall. The parent is often close by, looking appropriately concerned and often murmuring reminders that this is because the child did so-and-so, and she can come back when the time is up or when she stops crying.

By this point in my observations, I often tend to start crying as well. The sight and sound of a crying child being forced to be alone in his sadness is something that really bugs me and makes me feel very bad for both the child and the parents who think that this is the way to get their child to behave in a certain way. I cannot leave small children alone with emotions they don't yet know how to handle, no matter how uncomfortable I am with the emotions it brings up for me. Attachment parenting encourages us not to ignore the cries of a baby, and as children get older, they have more emotions and acquire more words, but they do not acquire *all* of the words we would like them to have. So they "cry" in different ways, and we have to—we are privileged to—take the time to learn these new cries. "Help me understand and negotiate the world," they are saying.

To me, time-outs work because no one wants to sit alone crying while facing a wall. I wouldn't want to, would you? And so a child learns to associate the "misbehavior" with the time-out, which is, in reality, a punishment—a withholding of activities, socializing, and attention. The child realizes that sitting and crying while facing a wall is no fun at all and she had best stop what she did to be put there. However, this teaches the child nothing about *why* the behavior was unwelcome, nor does it give motivation to internalize why to stop. Now, I know that parents do tend to tell children why they are being put in a time-out, and I also know that "You're going to get a time-out!" is heard as often at our local park as "Mommy, I need to pee." But the use of a threat of being alone and crying is not the motivation we want for our children to behave well, or to follow the rules and expectations we have of them. We want them to behave in a certain way because it feels right, makes sense to them, and makes for positive interactions with everyone around them.

Finally, just as we discussed cry-it-out methods of sleep training, I believe that it goes against our intuition and our instinct as parents to cause our children to cry and to deny them love and soothing. We convince ourselves that it is for their own good, but this logic makes sense only to an adult mind that has been influenced by a lot of professional parenting books and coaches. If you feel queasy when you force your child into a chair facing a wall, or when you shut him in his room and hear him wailing, sobbing, and choking on his tears through a closed door, know that this is not the only way to change undesirable behavior. Listening to your instincts can help you to bring that child back into your lap and into a world he can manage and understand better.

Threat and Reward

For the reasons I just discussed, threats work because no one wants the consequences that come after "If you don't . . . then I am going to. . . ." Threats are a power struggle where the parent always wins and the child can never win. Especially in the case of the illogical consequences that come after some threats, children can't win because they don't even understand the rules—and we parents usually don't understand them, either. Along the same lines, rewards work under a similar premise: the parent has the power and authority to decide what is good and what deserves a present, a cookie, a treat, or whatever.

Like time-outs, threats and rewards do seem to work, but they work for the wrong reasons. Just as children respond to threats because they fear the consequences, they also respond to rewards because it is the reward that is driving them, rather than being motivated by working well with others, earning respect, being valued, and being appreciated and loved. This is not to say that I have never used a lollipop to get my son to sit quietly with my husband at a wedding I was a bridesmaid in, because I indeed have done that and it worked, but it also felt a little bit weird.

And if we give a reward or a threat once or twice, we have not failed and we have not initiated a pattern that we will never break. You don't expect your child to be perfect, and you don't have to be a perfect parent, either. That's okay. Children are very flexible, and they will follow our lead at all stages of their development. So all is not lost if you slip once in a while; it simply should not be your principal mode of operating, or you may be encouraging desirable outcomes by undesirable methods. (For the record, I have never used that lollipop trick again.)

Violence

I have saved this one for last, because I find that it is the hardest of all the parenting tools to discuss. With all due respect to all styles of parenting, violence against a child baffles me. The only relationship in society in which you are allowed to hit or spank another person is the one with your child; you can't spank your husband or your wife. You can't spank your teachers or your friends, and you most certainly can't even adopt a pet in most states if you say that you plan to use spanking as a disciplinary measure. What is it about hitting children that has come to have such a sacred and almost revered quality in our society?

People who hit children often use the Bible as their reasoning; it is simply erroneous to do so, and for those who have studied the Bible's references to the "rod," you know that using the Bible as a defense of hitting smarts of sacrilege. People who hit children say that they hit out of love and not out of anger. The distinction between hitting in anger (as in "the heat of the moment") as opposed to hitting as part of a purportedly "calm," regimented spanking is an academic one but not a practical one; both methods involve hitting a child, thereby causing a tiny brain to release neurotransmitters and hormones to cope with pain and fear while suppressing fight/flight pathways. The simplest reason we don't hit is this: hitting is hitting. It's not love. It's not teaching. It's hitting. You can say you are hitting with love, or that you are using hitting to teach something, but it's still hitting.

How big of a problem is the use of physical punishment? According to Elizabeth T. Gershoff's 2008 report for the Phoenix Children's Hospital, a significantly large percentage of parents in the United States physically punish children, with research detailing that nearly two thirds of parents with children the age of two use physical punishment. By the time children reach fifth grade, 80 percent have been physically punished. By high school, 85 percent of adolescents report that they have been physically punished, with 51 percent reporting that they have been hit with a belt or something similar. Shockingly, the U.S. Department of Education's Office of Civil Rights reported that in the 2004–2005 school year, 272,028 public school children received physical punishment *in school*.

So is all of this physical punishment working? Well, research indicates that physical punishment fails to promote long-term compliance and is actually correlated with *less* internalization of appropriate behavior and compliance. In addition, many studies report that the more children receive physical punishment, the more defiant they are and the less likely they are to show empathy for others. Throughout the world, physical punishment is associated with increased psychological maladjustment and mental health problems such as anxiety and depression, as well as drug and alcohol abuse. Perhaps most disturbingly, people who experienced physical punishment as children are more likely to report having hit a boyfriend or girlfriend than those who have not been physically punished.

In Sweden, the first country to ban all physical punishment of children in 1979, the percentage of adults who hold positive attitudes toward spanking has declined from over 50 percent in the 1960s to 10 percent in 2000. Maybe it's that simple.

> Since 1979, twenty-four countries have formally made physical punishment unacceptable and illegal in all settings, including the home: Sweden (1979), Finland (1983), Norway (1987), Austria (1989), Croatia (1994), Cyprus (1994), Denmark (1997), Latvia (1998), Bulgaria (2000), Germany (2000), Israel (2000), Iceland (2003), Romania (2004), Ukraine (2004), Hungary (2005), Greece (2006), Chile (2007), the Netherlands (2007), New Zealand (2007), Portugal (2007), Uruguay (2007), Spain (2007), Venezuela (2007), and Costa Rica (2008).

Hitting doesn't work.

People who hit children sometimes claim it's the only way to get them to behave, and they modify these statements with three phrases. I would like to address each of these claims in turn.

1. *"I have wild/hyper/crazy kids."* Gentle discipline and using methods other than violence against your child are appropriate for every kind of child, no matter their temperament. There is no such thing as a child who deserves to be hit, or who cannot be parented without being hit. In some cases, an assessment by a child psychiatrist may be helpful, but hitting does not help children whom you already deem as difficult; in fact, it may make things worse.

2. *"I am too overwhelmed to do it any other way."* The commitment not to hit your children works if you have one child or if you have ten. If you cannot handle the stress of having a large family without using physical violence to keep it all together and running smoothly, perhaps a larger family than what you presently

have is not the best option for you, and a skilled therapist, mid-wife, obstetrician, or clergyperson can help you work through it if limiting your desire for a larger family is problematic for you. An adult's lack of resources and support is not the fault of a child, and children do not deserve to be hit because we are stressed out. The times when I have felt the most like I might hit my children have been times when they were not doing anything "bad" or "evil." Rather, *I* was exhausted, *I* was at the end of my rope in terms of patience and resources, and *I* needed to get anger and frustration out of my body. These are precisely the times *not* to hit a child. These are the times to realize that *we* need help so that we do not use our children as essentially a punching bag.

3. *"It's how I was raised and I turned out fine."* Many people you know were hit as children and many turned out seemingly fine. Some believe they deserved to be hit and don't know why others can't just "get over it." As a neuroscientist trained in cognitive neuropsychology, I have come to the conclusion that, to put it simply, every child reacts differently to being hit. Some grow up and don't think much about it, and they lead perfectly fine lives. Critics of harsh discipline might purport that the internal psyche of a hit child will show indications of distress, but to the outside world, many such people function well. However, there are some children whose neurochemical makeup and psychological profile does not respond this way to being hit. These children are deeply wounded and often traumatized by experiences at the hands of parents, and they can never quite shake off the feelings those experiences aroused.

When we look at our newborns for the first time, there is no stamp that they come with saying, "I'll be okay—hit away!" or "I'm not going to be okay—don't hit me!" You don't know which kind of child you are getting. Is it worth the risk that your hitting will lead them to become the kind of teenager and adult who can't understand the pain they experienced? The negative effects may present in school, social relationships, sexual relationships, confidence, work, and overall mental health. I ask again: is it worth risking all of that?

Children are born trusting us to love them and protect them. We teach them right from wrong. We save them from pain and shield them from danger. No matter how much we rationalize our reasons for hitting, a child will never—*never*—be able to either consciously or unconsciously reconcile that the person who is their parent is deliberately causing them pain, fear, and terror.

Any lab animal will recoil from physical pain, and it will demonstrate both the physical and neurological signs of fear, such as cowering, freezing, shaking, hiding, and crying. Repeated presentations of the thing or person who caused the pain will eventually lead the animal to show these displays of fear and terror upon seeing the thing or person. Meaning: after a few times of being hurt by someone, even a rodent will learn to fear that person. The animal may try to run away or hide, or may simply freeze and act . . . obedient. Hitting as a form of discipline is, in actuality, conditioning your child with pain, fear, and terror. We intuitively want our children to listen to us, to learn from us, and to model our behavior. We do not want them to fear us as the motivation for their "good" behavior. It's not worth it.

What Works

Here's what we have found works for our family within the framework of gentle discipline.

Always assume the best.

All children have the potential to be sweet, cooperative, helpful, kind, and loving. Does this mean that they always are? No. Does this mean that they *can* be? Yes. Try to start each day knowing that somewhere inside even the unhappiest child, there is the seed of a child who can grow into a happy one who meets your expectations and then exceeds them. This can be done, though, only when we foster that growth. As a new parent, I sometimes felt that I did something very wrong to make our little guys angry, sad, moody, or defiant, especially as they entered toddlerhood. I came to realize that I—the adult—needed to see past outward expressions of what I perceived as negative behaviors in order to find out how to allow our guys to be their best. This is something that really revolutionized my perception of our kids, and I often find myself overwhelmed with love and gratitude for our boys even in their "darker" or less desirable moments.

See "bad" behavior as a sign of an unmet need.

When children act out, disobey us, behave rudely, or display disturbing emotions, it's easy to dismiss them or the behavior as "bad" or "wrong." Indeed, throwing things in anger, cursing, lying, stealing, and physical violence are generally looked down upon by most people in society, as they should be. However, as we go about redirecting our children and disciplining them, it helps tremendously to see these behaviors as a child's best attempt to meet a need. This does not mean we simply frame stealing candy, for example, as a need for candy. Rather, children often "act out" to get attention, to get love or affection, or to meet needs they themselves may not even understand. This does not excuse the behavior, but it should make us pause before we use punitive measures to stop it. Instead, it calls upon us to look at our relationship with our child to try and find the source of the unmet need.

When Miles has had his moments of irrational behavior, fits of rage, and uncontrollable anger and sadness that would make a strong adult want to cry as well, I have tried to see that, as a child, he has a limited verbal vocabulary, and he has a limited emotional one as well. Identifying one's own needs and having them met efficiently are skills that take practice and refinement. (I know many adults who haven't gotten this right yet!) Perhaps by our seeing our children as being in need of learning this skill, they will become adults who are able to practice it in their own relationships with success and satisfaction.

Detach from your child's behavior.

We can all relate to this scenario: you are in line for a movie, play, or amusement park ride, and your kid wants something. Pick what your kid would want: a hot dog, candy bar, plastic toy from a coin machine, whatever. You say no, and your kid proceeds to throw a total fit. Embellish as needed: he may throw his little body onto the pavement, scream, curse, hit; use whatever details you like to really paint that picture of a hissy fit in the middle of everything and everyone. In this imagined scenario, were you not surrounded by strangers, you might let the tantrum proceed on its course until your child is done, or until he is distracted, since some people find that ignoring these kinds of outbursts does the trick for their kid. However, instead of ignoring this fit, you glance around at the other people in line and see that they are annoyed with your kid's shrieking; who wouldn't be? They are rolling their eyes. You are certain that you hear the young engaged couple in front of you decide they will never have kids "because of that monster child behind us." Maybe your in-laws are on line with you and they accuse you of being a doormat by putting up with totally inappropriate behavior. So what do you do? You react poorly. Harshly. Angrily. Maybe even violently.

How many times have we acted more harshly with our children in front of others than we might if we were alone with them because we were embarrassed by the scene they were making and didn't want to be seen as "soft"? We've all done it, but it is important to realize that your child is not a direct reflection of your goodness as a person. Sometimes kids freak out and have hissy fits and there is little we can do. Maybe you are holding firm to a rule you have established, such as no candy before dinner, or maybe you have a spirited kid who reacts in big ways to even seemingly small things and you know that she will be fine once she screams for a minute or ten. Either way, trust that your parental license will not be revoked if others think you are not a good parent.

Parent time-outs

Let's go back to the previous example of the hissy fit. This time, imagine that you are home or in the car. Now imagine that you cannot contain your disdain for the way your child is behaving. Maybe it's been a particularly stressful day; maybe the request that he is making is too much for you to handle; maybe you just have a distinct sense that you are on the verge of doing or saying something you will no doubt regret.

This is when it's time for a parent time-out. People do this in many ways. If you have older children, you can simply say you are having a hard time and need a moment to gather yourself. Some people add that they feel out of control and do not want to do or say something that would hurt their child, but that should be done only with a child who can comprehend this kind of discussion. You then need to either physically take a moment or hone the skill of taking a time-out in the child's presence, using breathing techniques or some sort of mantra or short meditation.

I learned a relaxation exercise in Dr. Ilene Val-Essen's Quality Parenting class that has significantly helped me lower my general state of aggravation and tension. The best thing about it is that it takes about ninety seconds to do, it can be done standing up, sitting down, in the shower, while brushing your teeth, or in between the front door of your house and the car. Incredibly, any time I do it, it helps, and the feelings this exercise brings me can be summoned throughout the day, whenever I feel my tension rising and my frustration building. It's sort of been the magic wand in my parenting, and I try to do it in the morning in between waking up and getting out of bed, typically while nursing Fred and being jumped on by Miles, but it works just the same.

1. Inhale, imagining negative energy leaving your belly and moving up through your heart, through your throat, and into your head.
2. Hold the breath for five seconds, imagining the negative energy being transformed into positive energy.
3. Exhale and picture the energy leaving through the space between your eyes, releasing any tension there and filling the room with the positive energy you just made.
4. Take a deep breath, acknowledging that you just turned negative energy into positive energy.
5. Repeat two more times.

A parent time-out is not a punishment, nor is it intended to communicate to a child that her behavior is pushing you away. It is important to make your intentions clear to your child: that you are unable to talk more or discuss anything further without cooling down. (For more on Dr. Val-Essen's work, see the Resources section.)

Compare organic locally grown Fuji apples to organic locally grown Fuji apples.

There is no child exactly like yours and there is no family exactly like yours. Have you heard the expression "Compare apples to apples, and not apples to oranges"? Well, wondering why so-and-so's kid (an orange) sits so nicely in a high chair, eats bok choy without a complaint, "never" cries, makes his own breakfast, and won the cutest-child-of-the-year contest in the local county fair three years in a row is not only ridiculous (isn't there some rule about winning it more than two years in a row?), but it will only hurt you and your child (an apple) as well. Measuring your child's behavior (or misbehavior) by another child is destructive and frustrating for all involved. Your family is its own little universe, and what works for your family may not work for others' families, and vice versa.

I would suggest not to even compare a particular child of yours to a sibling, even if they are identical twins! Every child is a specific and special human being with specific and special needs and desires. Treat your children that way, and take it one step beyond not comparing apples to oranges; avoid even comparing two apples from the same barrel.

Be gentle with yourself.

When you decided to have children, did you take a test that assessed your perfection as a person that you passed with flying colors? You didn't? Good, I didn't, either. Truth be told, there is no such test for perfection that gives us the green light to become a parent knowing that we will always do things perfectly. In addition, there is no guarantee that even if we were perfect in every way that our children would turn out perfect in every way as well. Part of our journey on this earth for the short time that we are here is to do our best to make the world a better place. As parents, we get to pursue this task as we try to help our children reach their potential, while learning how to make ourselves better people at the same time. No one expects you or your children to be perfect, and being hard on yourself only breaks your resolve and weakens your abilities to help your children achieve their potential in their lives.

If you fall short of your ideal as a parent, this does not mean that gentle discipline doesn't work, or that you are too overwhelmed, too high-strung, too damaged, or too impatient to parent this way. It simply means that you need more help and support (see chapter 13 on achieving the balance in your life that can help you be more gentle with yourself). Be as gentle with yourself as you hope to be with your child, and if that doesn't work, be as gentle with yourself as you would want a stranger, teacher, or future life partner to be with your child.

Commonly used tools to encourage you to be gentle with yourself:

1. When you feel particularly burned out, go easy on chores or checking things off your list of things to accomplish; order dinner in or make a simple meal rather than adding the stress of cooking and preparing to your plate.

2. Find simple and inexpensive ways to relax, such as reading for pleasure, drinking a cup of tea while sitting down quietly, or taking a hot bath without being interrupted. (I used to sneak in a ten-minute bath as soon as both boys were asleep so I'd be finished before Fred woke up for his first nursing.)

3. Meditative practices such as yoga increase your overall patience and reserves of emotional strength by lowering your blood pressure and encouraging you to exercise the "emotional muscles" of being calm and centered.

Our Favorite Discipline Tools

I am grateful to my husband for encouraging and supporting the path of gentle discipline as the only way to raise our children. He has stopped me many times from doing and saying things I know I would regret, and for that our children and I thank him. We are by no means always calm, always serene, or ever "perfect," but we have a system that seeks to stop short of things that we know would cause a rift in the fabric of our relationship with our boys. Here are some of our favorite tools.

"Not for" instead of "no"

From the second I even looked pregnant with our first son, I was warned by people that my kid, at some point, probably in his first year of life, was going to make me nuts by saying/shouting/scream-ing, "NO!"

Thanks, I would think, *I can't wait.* We took a Parent & Me class through our local Waldorf school when our first son was eleven months old. Our brilliant teacher really helped form our identity as parents, and one of the things she taught us was why the word "no" is not helpful and will, in fact, come back to haunt you. We heeded her advice and used the word "no" very rarely, instead com-ing up with a myriad of ways to indicate "no" to stop undesirable behaviors, using "Not for Miles" a lot. We never baby-proofed our home except for power-outlet covers, and "Not for Miles" saved us so much time and energy as he crawled toward wires and lamps but never hurt himself or broke one item in our home. When something was dangerous, a stern tone (which we saved for only such occa-sions) and strong body language did the trick in averting his explora-tion of dangerous things.

As he got older and we started to teach such lessons as not draw-ing on furniture and not touching foods that were not good for his digestive tract, "Not for Miles" worked again. One of his first words was "not-not," which meant "Not for Miles." And to this day, neither of my boys have ever said, shouted, or screamed "NO!" at us, nor have they screamed "NOT FOR!" in its place. Just as we demonstrated for them many creative and nonpunitive ways to have limits, so, too, did they make up many creative ways to show their limits.

Possessives, *not possession*

The second thing people told me when I was pregnant was, "Just wait until the 'mine!' phase. Just you wait!" Since the "no" thing went so well, we applied the same logic to a child's natural desire for possession, which they typically express with "MINE!" We named objects with possess*ives* rather than with possess*ion*. At the park, instead of "That's *his*; this is *yours*" (which would inevitably lead a child to think, *This is mine!*), we would say, "That's the one he is using, this is Miles's." Or at the dinner table, "This is Mama's food, and this is Miles's food." And wouldn't you know it, we never had a "Mine!" phase with either of our boys. Do they want things for themselves? Of course! Do they tug at each other's toys and push each other to see who will get the toy by force? Absolutely! This usually happens at least ten times just by 8 a.m.! But when the word "mine" is removed from the power struggle, it makes room for discussion and communication even if children are not fully verbal, and that's something that is *mine* to celebrate.

Give a yes for every no, sometimes two.

There are times when we need to and ought to say no to a child. Examples that spring to mind are when my boys wanted to touch my breasts in public, or when a slice of someone's brightly colored fantastic-looking birthday cake is asked for but is not vegan, or when my sweet toddler basically asked me to fabricate a coin-operated car in a mall where there simply was not one around. Saying no is always hard for me, and saying no sometimes makes people cry. I don't like to make people cry. Giving in to crying reinforces both my inability to be the parent and set the limits I need to set, and it also defeats the purpose of saying no in the first place.

What I have discovered is that small people love to hear "yes" even if it's after "no." Even if it's a really disappointing "no," I have found that providing a "yes" to something else can work wonders. So if touching my breasts is not okay, I provide a few choices of touching that are okay. "You cannot touch my breasts, but you can hold my arm, kiss my cheek, or hold your water bottle." As for the nonvegan cake, this "no" is sometimes one of the hardest to conquer, but we always travel with vegan treats to birthday parties so that even if the answer is "no" to the exciting cake, the answer is "yes" to our own treat (which is sometimes a whole-wheat organic bran muffin, but neither of my kids needs to know that). If I am asked to fabricate a coin-operated car in a mall, the "yes" may look like this: "I can't give you the car you want, but we can take a super fast ride in the shopping cart in the parking lot, or we can have a crazy piggy-back ride to the car." Sometimes the crying does not cease, but most times it has.

This kind of flexibility and creativity allows your children to see you as not perfect, but perfectly happy to do your best to make them comfortable in uncomfortable situations. It also prevents me from feeling like I am constantly saying no, because I'm all of a sudden not saying no all of the time!

Show me one.

Transitions are hard for little people. Some have a harder time than others, but generally speaking, when a child (or an adult, for that matter) is having fun, it's hard to stop and go home. When transitions began to be sticky for our boys, my husband thought of an ingenious trick, which to this day remains my favorite. As soon as they were old enough (somewhere around eighteen months), we would signal the end of an event, a meal, or a ball game by having them "show me one." We taught them that "one" meant holding up one tiny chunky finger and making eye contact. And they learned very quickly that once they held up that little tiny chunky finger and had "one more," we picked up and went home. It has literally worked for us every time, no tantrums, no refusing to leave, no begging for more bites of dessert.

As a neuroscientist, I have felt a compulsive need to know why this works—maybe it's something about the mental distraction of holding up the finger? I don't know; I really have no clue, but we use it for every situation we can think of to apply it to and it works. During a french fry–eating episode when he was just under two, Fred held up an index finger on *both* hands to indicate that he wanted more than just "one more." He knew it was funny, and I almost wanted to let him have "two more" for his clever effort, but I smiled instead and said, "not two more, Fred; one more." He smiled back and understood. As Fred got older, we taught him this phrase: "one and then done." He finds this so much fun to say that he seems to forget he wanted more than one!

Distraction/humor

The way we discouraged undesirable behavior when our older son was starting to get into everything within reach was with a healthy dose of distraction—not distraction from feelings, but physical distraction. So instead of baby proofing and stapling wires to walls, we redirected his reaching body toward objects that were better suited for him than a phone cord or piece of cat food or bird poop on the pavement. And instead of spending a lot of time negotiating with him and explaining over and over why he was too small to climb some things, we distracted him with something to climb that *was* his size. This worked extremely well, and he soon became very motivated to spend time pursuing things that he could have fun with without a lot of struggle.

As he turned four, though, sweet Miles began to exhibit some behaviors that we were quite unfamiliar with. We had heard about these behaviors from friends who had had spirited one-year-olds, rambunctious two-year-olds, and feisty three-year-olds. Our son was none of those things at those ages, so this was new to us. He was angry when things didn't go his way, aggressive, and he started making very disturbing growling sounds and really intimidating scowling faces. It was kind of funny, but it was also not funny at all. We read a book that suggested distracting with humor and we tried it. Within seconds, ridiculous outlandish humor could lift his anger and frustration and lighten his mood.

An example: if he was crying about wanting to play outside when it was dinnertime and bedtime, instead of engaging in long conversations about the value of dinner and bed (which he could have cared less about), we would say something like "I know! Let's move to the moon where it's never dinnertime or bedtime and you can be elected president and decide to play all day!" Silly? Yes? Nonsensical? Absolutely. Made him instantly stop crying and go to the dinner table? Case closed.

We return to this distraction-with-humor technique when the world is bigger than he wants it to be, and when he exhibits signs that he wants to be big but doesn't yet know how to be, which is really frustrating and scary for him. Thank goodness for humor, because he now uses it on us, and it sometimes is just the trick to distract us from our frustrations, too.

Give up all reasoning.

Speaking of children who turn four, that was the age when my dear intellectual husband decided that our son needed to also become an intellectual. My husband would spend more minutes with Miles than I have had alone with him in years discussing the merits of not throwing pillows at his baby brother's head. They would sit on the couch, Miles staring straight ahead as if in a trance, with my dear husband repeating again and again in every way he could possibly imagine how it's not nice to do that to Fred, and Fred is a baby with a very heavy head but poor neck support due to the underdeveloped musculature in an infant, blah blah blah.

This went on for a few months, and my husband used his powers of reasoning every time he could, because it's just how he operates and he assumed Miles would operate that way as well. Bright as I would like to think our son is, he did *not* seem to understand any of it. In general, I don't like to tell my husband how to parent, but I couldn't take this reasoning lesson anymore. I finally broke down and told my husband that adult reasoning wasn't working for Miles. "But how will he ever learn?" he asked. "I'm not sure, but not that way," I responded.

What we have settled on is that small doses of age-appropriate definitions and explanations that focus on cause and effect do seem to work very well. For example, "Throwing pillows at baby Fred is scary for him and it could hurt him. Pillows are for sleeping on, so I am going to ask you to help me put them back on the bed, but not on Fred's head." There will be plenty of time for reasoning, but not now.

Pick your battles/Do you want to die on this mountain?/Let it go.

I am not a permissive parent; I hope you can trust me on this by now. However, a very effective tool I have used possibly more than any other as a parent is this: pick your battles, especially with a baby. Ask yourself, "Do I want to die on this mountain?" and answer it very honestly. Know that sometimes you just have to let stuff go and that this does not doom your child to a lifetime of bad behavior. It simply means that you acknowledge that every phase is just that: it's a phase, and it will pass. And it will usually pass with you doing very little to fix it; maturity, experience, and observing good modeling of behavior is often enough to correct undesirable behavior.

Take throwing plates off of high chairs (the baby, not you). When our sons did this, it made me nuts. I tried picking the plate up and putting it back on the tray, stating very seriously that I was not going to do it again. And guess what? They'd invariably throw it again, this time with a smile! I tried looking disappointed and hurt. That did nothing. What I finally did was ask parents whom I respected, and they all said the same thing: let it go; it will pass. And so I did, and it did. I didn't pay much attention to the plate throwing. When it happened after three or so times, I gently said, "All done," and I put it away. And they were almost always done by then, so that worked out well.

We used the same nonreactivity to our boys' learning how loud they could shout or playing with their food. Certain behaviors, such as a baby who bites while nursing or a child who thinks it is funny to pull hair, need a different kind of guidance, but for most things that are challenging but not truly problematic, I say let it go and you will be amazed that it passes. You don't have to punish a baby for it to pass. I am here to tell you that it passes on its own.

My Child, My Friend

In my experience, the passion with which parents debate discipline techniques is unmatched by any other aspect of parenting. Although there are many ways to apply disciplinary measures with our children, it is important for us to set limits without compromising our dignity, our child's rights, or our intuition. Gentle discipline offers that however you choose to run your house, coming from a place of respect, empathy, and loving guidance will forge a relationship with your child that will surpass that of just parent and child. Using gentle discipline has the potential to make your child your friend in childhood and adulthood while still maintaining your boundaries and limits. Hurting a child with your words, your thoughts, and your deeds can stay with her forever.

I strongly encourage you to read an entire book describing gentle discipline (see the Resources section), and hear from real parents both what it looks like to make the switch, and what it looks like to reap the benefits of parenting this way. Gentle discipline can work for every child and every parent, if only we invest the time and energy to make it happen with consistency, authenticity, and love. And that is, quite simply, the most intuitive way to discipline and to be.

Part IV

What Mommy Needs

12

Keeping Your Relationships Strong: Staying "You" When You Become a Parent

Parenting presents a tall order: your baby has a lot of needs and wants, and it is your job to provide them, especially if you choose a style of parenting that falls under the umbrella term "attachment parenting." The needs and wants of a young baby and child are seemingly endless, and babies clearly don't know that especially around 7 p.m., you would like them to stop needing and wanting so much! If you were raised in Western culture or with any knowledge of progressive psychology, by now you must be thinking, *What about me and my needs?!* Or perhaps more appropriately, "If I don't get five minutes to myself I am going to scream disturbingly loud and throw tonight's not-yet-finished dinner out of the nearest window and everyone can just eat crackers and candy bars for dinner! *Okay?*"

Don't worry; I haven't forgotten about what *parents* need in all of this parenting business. Living in accordance with the principles of attachment parenting does not dictate a life in which your needs are not important. Balancing your needs with those of your child is what a responsible parent does. It's normal to feel the tug of the tension of that balance, and it's okay to feel more than one emotion at once. Being a parent is exhilarating and beautiful, but at the same time it is also challenging and frustrating.

Children need healthy parents. Children need sane parents. Children need parents who value themselves and their well-being. It's what makes us truly available to our children: knowing that our needs are met allows us to give everything we've got to meet our children's needs. People who encourage their children's needs to dictate a household are doing their children a disservice by setting them up for a world where they feel entitled to everything they desire, even at the expense of others' needs. We want our children to both know that their needs are met and to see a model of healthy parents who can get their own needs met, too. As we have discussed, the expectation of your needs may need to shift significantly once you make these attachment-friendly parenting choices, but that does not mean that your needs get thrown away entirely.

You should know (or remind yourself if you once knew and have since forgotten) that as a parent, you have not become lost, drifting on a sea of baby, never to find solid ground among your friends and your spouse again. You are still important. It is important to talk with other adults about things not related to babies or children. It is important to feel that life can reward you—even in small ways—with a special meal or outing with someone you care about. It is important to foster relationships and to maintain romance and intimacy in your marital situation. No one wants a cranky, angry, resentful parent, and I can guarantee you (from some pretty rough trial and error) that not talking to other adults, not feeling any small perk from life, not fostering friendships, and not maintaining romance and intimacy in your marriage are surefire ways to demonstrate what a *not* sane mama looks like. Fortunately, children recover from our moments of frustration when we return to them genuinely and sincerely with love and affection and take measures to not repeat the same mistakes again. However, we need to take feeling isolated, out of touch with our relationships, and stale and exhausted in our marriage as signs that we need to get our relationship needs met more efficiently and consistently.

There are many ways to recharge your relationship battery and remind yourself that you matter. I will avoid listing the things I would do with unlimited funds and caregivers for our boys besides me and my husband, since I don't have unlimited funds or a desire for any caregiver besides me and my husband. As an aside, these fantasy things would include frequent trips to the spa with friends, a gym and yoga studio membership that I would use at least three times a week, taking a class at a local college on a topic I enjoy learning about, and dinner out with friends twice a week. I would also like to go to a foreign movie with my husband and discuss it afterward over a glass of wine and some chocolate cake, but that might put me over the edge of indulgence, so we'll just leave that aside for now!

I am going to give you some guidelines for maintaining your relationships and some of the ways that I have tried to maintain sanity as an adult when my days and world sometimes seem to really be about activities and interactions where I am the tallest person and the only one capable of peeing and washing my hands all by myself with no one helping me.

Disclaimer: Keep in mind that I am in no way perfect or even close to it on these matters; I am simply sharing the best advice I have been given that has worked for me in theory, if not totally in practice yet. (My husband is standing over me as I type this, and he really wants you to know I am not perfect in this area. Thank you, dear.)

Things to Forget

One of my best suggestions when approaching this issue of the needs of an adult who has relationships with other adults once you become a parent is to simply and as unemotionally as possible *forget what life used to look like.* The days of sleeping in, running to get Indian food at midnight with your girlfriends/spouse before driving to Vegas with no hotel reservation waiting for you are *over.* I repeat: *over.* The days of hours and hours of fantastic, loud experimental sex that involved more than one room of the house? Also over. And the days of having nothing to do but lounge around, eat french fries, watch TV, and nap? Absolutely 100 percent over, over, over. Over. I mean it. Over.

Does this mean life will never be fun, spontaneous, or make you feel alive again? No. It simply means that it will be different, and your expectations need to be realistic or you will be majorly bummed out. There is a lot to enjoy and find joy in when you are a parent, and attempts to make your life look like it did before will either fail miserably or result in your child not getting the most and best of you. Recall also that the first weeks and months as a parent are the hardest, so don't feel discouraged if you feel like your entire life (not just the social aspect) is over. It will get fun again, both with kids and with your friends and spouse without kids around. I promise!

As I recommended in the introduction, it is very important to *forget other people's opinions* regarding your decisions about how to have (or not have) a social life because of your parenting decisions. Many well-meaning friends, family, and random acquaintances or even strangers on the street love tell me how damaging it is for me not to get out once in a while, go away for trips with my girlfriends, or have romantic getaways with my husband. These people like to get right up in my face, as it were, and say, with a seriousness that startles me even in my most self-assured moments, "Happy children need a happy mom." Or "Sacrificing your own needs only makes you resentful, doesn't it?" And "Is your husband on board with all of this?"

My husband and I have each come up with different ways to handle this. Truth be told, I often get defensive and find myself doubting our choices, but my husband is very helpful in bringing me back to reality. He has no problem looking people right in the eye with a friendly smile and declaring, "We're doing what's best for our family" or "We have full confidence in our choices." What he has taught me is that I need to have my own phrases handy and well practiced for the times when people invariably question our parenting and, specifically, how it relates to our relationship.

If it's about my kids' well-being: "They're happy, rested, well fed, and secure. It's working for us."

If it's about insinuations of deprivation: "There will come a time again for retreats and spa weekends, I know it. For now, this is what life looks like and we're happy with it."

If it's about being out of touch: "Thank goodness for email, Facebook, Netflix, and getting my news off the Internet."

And if it's about my sex life, humor works: "We don't have energy to have that much sex anymore anyway." Or better yet: "We're like rabbits—it's nonstop action in our house!"

The more confident you can be (or at least sound), the more this way of parenting will become accepted as within the range of normal, healthy, and enjoyable—which it is! There is of course a time and a place to air complaints and brainstorm about ways to feel fulfilled, connected to people, and satisfied with your choices; you just need to go to the right place to get that support. Make it a personal goal to not care what others think of you and you will have a lot less conflict about your choices.

Friendships Matter

I am a person who has a lot of friends and acquaintances. And I meet new people all the time with whom I enjoy talking. I am not going to lie to you: having kids and parenting the way we do has put a real damper on my friendships. I simply do not have the time or energy to keep up all of the relationships I once so enjoyed. There was a serious period of adjustment for me once I became a mom. I could no longer field phone calls from a friend in need on my way to coffee with another friend and then have dinner with three more friends and then drinks with another group of friends. My social life truly came to a screeching halt when I had my first son, and it hasn't really been the same since.

Some aspects of this change clarified a lot about myself. I love being helpful to people and I am happy to be a shoulder for a friend to cry on. I love to give advice when it is asked for, and I know I can be a really good listener and friend. But I also need to take care of my life and my own needs, and this became the most clear when I became a mom. In my new role, a tiny someone needed me as a friend and companion more than anyone else in the whole world, and it was my job to be there for that little person over and above anyone else. Wow. That was a huge reality check.

As empowering and fantastic as this new responsibility was, I also honestly missed the days of hanging out with girlfriends over tea, whispering about cute waiters at trendy restaurants, and visiting my favorite funky clothing boutiques when they had sales. These were activities I really enjoyed, and a part of me missed those things even in my most content moments as a mom. I found that denying my needs only made them stronger. I learned to talk about this conflict and to express out loud the sense of loss I felt at not being able to continue the relationships and activities I used to enjoy the way I used to enjoy them.

While expressing this was good, it also could make me feel,

frankly, down. I felt myself becoming resentful and I started doubting my choices. I would snap at my husband and sometimes I was short with my kids, even when they were too young to understand what I was annoyed about. These were not good days. These are what my wise La Leche leader calls evidence of Mama "running on fumes." "When Mama ain't happy, ain't nobody happy" is also how she put it. I have found this to be true.

For me, running on fumes is usually an indication that I need to recharge my battery. What are the things I have found I can do to accomplish this? It's not a secret that my life changed significantly when I became a mom, but for too long I tried to pretend that nothing had changed. This was not a good plan, because my make-believe world was so far from the reality that it was a bit like "The Emperor's New Clothes." (No matter how hard the Emperor tried to act as though he was not naked, he, in fact, was very naked, and everyone knew it!)

So the first thing I do with my friends is to be honest with them. And in the process, I get to be honest with myself (bonus!). How am I honest? I express my frustrations when I'm with my friends without asking them to "fix" the choices I have made. For example, if I am invited to something that I simply cannot attend, I don't lie about why I can't attend it. I say, "I am really sorry I can't make it. I don't have child care for that time, and my husband is already playing ball with his friends that day." A lot of people, especially those who don't have children yet, are annoyed with our choices, and they express their frustration at my limited social life. I listen patiently, and I say that I understand that they are allowed to miss me and they are also allowed to have their own opinions. But it doesn't mean that I am doing anything wrong.

The second thing I do to recharge my battery may sound like a no-brainer, but it wasn't to me: I make sure to find time to have conversations by phone or email when I am not simultaneously doing five other things. Sometimes the best way for me to stay in touch with friends is to catch up by phone or email, but no one likes to feel that they can't listen (or be listened to) so I try to—*try to*—limit phone calls made while I am watching the kids to nuts-and-bolts types of talks rather than conversations of content. Monitoring my kids as they wrestle each other about the house, screaming and giggling, while attempting to find out how a girlfriend's biopsy of the mole she had removed last week went is not considerate to anyone involved, and it is downright frustrating as well.

As many friends as I had before I had kids, I have made more since having kids. I allowed myself to make new friends in our community even though I already thought I had too many friends to keep up with. I even found the resources to start my own moms' group with a few like-minded mamas (whose wisdom, shared experience, and struggles formed the basis for my parenting decisions, philosophy, and this book). Why? Because I needed a new kind of friend now.

I needed friends who spoke my parenting language, and it took some effort, but we formed a really nice group and have all decided to homeschool together. We even take turns with child care now that our kids are older. We have formed friendships as adults that will likely last throughout our lives. To try to make my before-kids friends, who parented differently, fit the needs I had as I started parenting this way was not fair to them or me. Of course, there are many things I can do with the friends I had before kids even if natural birth, breastfeeding, co-sleeping, elimination communication, and gentle discipline are not their choices, but it's also important for me to know that it's okay to make new friends who can be on this journey with me while maintaining older friendships and appreciating them all.

Romantic Relationships Matter

Nurturing a relationship with your spouse that stays fresh, romantic, and inspiring is very challenging, no matter your parenting style.

But I will say that when you choose to be the primary caregiver for your children for the first block of their lives, your ability to go out on dates and away for the weekend are nonexistent. As for me and my husband, a romantic, sexual, and even intellectual connection is sustained mostly when our children are sleeping. We have found a few television shows we watch together every television season, and we also invested in a large enough television so that we can watch movies while stretched out, sometimes with the baby asleep at the breast as we watch. (A good popcorn popper is also recommended.) Sweets and chocolate are things we love in moderation but don't want our boys having access to on any regular basis, so my husband and I like to enjoy these with our television watching to make it fun. Does this sound like an overly simplistic and juvenile way to have fun for people who used to love hours of raquetball, camping, hiking, and backpacking through Europe and the Middle East? Yes. But is it what's working now? Yes.

Something that my husband and I have had to accept is that we can't do the things together that we used to, but we can do *versions* of those things and find some joy in that. For example, we were racquetball partners before we started dating. Throughout our friendship and continuing during our courtship, we loved doing competitive sports together. Although it's not quite the same, we have found some ways to satisfy our desire for this physical outlet.

The first is to incorporate our competitive nature into games we play with our boys. As we play with our sons, we impress upon them the importance of Mama and Dada demonstrating their skills a little bit, too. They love to see us being playful, and it allows them to see a different side of us than they usually see, which mostly involves us making food, doing errands, and, as our older son puts it, making him "our slave"—by asking him to help clean up the house, which by his description of the task, he is clearly reluctant to do! We find simple joy in volleying a ball back and forth in the living room, or making up diving games in a pool when we swim at my folks'. It may sound ridiculous, but we have found a good source of fun again and it's helped our relationship a lot.

Another thing my husband and I have been discussing enjoying (but to be honest, we have not quite perfected with any regularity) is the world of workouts on the television that we can do side by side. Again, this satisfies our desire to be physical, and also allows us to tap in to our past shared recreational likes. Again: sounds silly? Yes. Works for us? Let's hope so.

We have also found creative ways to enjoy the things that defined us as a couple before kids. We used to love camping. With kids, it is much harder, but we have found that it has been worth the extra packing and planning (and stress!) to experience what we truly love about camping: being outside, sleeping beneath the stars, living simply for a few days at a time, and roughing it. We have found that our boys fall asleep very easily after a day of hiking and playing, and we get time together around a campfire, sitting and talking with no distractions, which at home include the phone, the computer, and the television. It's not perfect, but it's getting there.

As for keeping romance alive, this is something that is a constant work in progress. Romance has shifted a lot since we had kids. It sometimes means allowing your partner the space to be alone, sleep late, or go out with friends while the other handles bedtime solo. That's a far cry from sexy lingerie, rose petals in a bathtub, or a fancy French dinner with a good game of footsie, but once we had kids, we started to realize that what often ignites our passion for the other is when my husband or I shows compassion and understanding of our stresses and struggles to stay sane amid chaos. And it turns out that can be pretty appealing and attractive.

My husband and I used to love going out to eat in quiet grown-up places, and that luxury pretty much disappeared when we had kids. We can now go out to family-type places, but it's sort of a mad countdown from the second we walk in the door to see who melts down first: the kids or us. Between taking the kids to the bathroom, spilled water, food that isn't liked as well as we all hoped it would be, and our younger son, who will repeatedly announce over and over after three bites of food, "Me done me done me done me dooooone," it's just not at all relaxing or enjoyable. Eating special meals at home is something we try to do with more regularity, and the Jewish Sabbath, which we observe, encourages special and elaborate meals every Friday night and Saturday, no matter what the week has looked like. This is something I especially look forward to since having kids, because it's a reminder that food can still matter and that presentation and the company at the table all add up to a special experience. I can wear my fuzzy slippers the whole time, and if anyone melts down, a glass of wine and the bedroom are close by.

Attention to your partner's physical appearance can get tricky once you have kids. Trust me: when we got married, my husband could not have known what I would look like after sleeping no more than an hour at a time for weeks on end. He also probably could not have pictured what I would look—or smell—like after not showering for four days because a very sick child had literally been attached to my body for that long. And I am 100 percent certain that he could not have anticipated what my stomach would look like after having two large babies.

However (and this goes for wives as well as husbands), to be sincerely told that you *are* attractive and desirable remains a very tender, special moment between lovers throughout a relationship. I do not expect my husband to go on and on about how stunning I look as I go to the park in my schleppy "mama park attire," but I really value the times when he can identify that I have made an effort to look put together. It also reminds me that it is still important to look put together for myself! And I try to remember that he also needs to be told he is still attractive to me. The sparks of romance may not be the same once you have kids, but the fire can still be kindled, if only for a flash here and there. Those flashes will eventually build again the bonfire you once knew.

I have also found that once you have kids, your partner needs a whole new set of vocabulary that includes many expressions of gratitude, understanding, and letting go of the need to control everything about how the kids are raised. Nothing kills romance more than constantly being nagged at, and that goes for both partners. In addition, because you are tackling things you never have before you had kids, being very specific about what you appreciate or value in your partner as a parent helps establish a strong foundation of love and trust that is the basis for a good romantic and intimate connection. Everyone likes to hear that he is doing a great job, that he handled that wicked tantrum very skillfully, that you can see he is struggling but the kids are lucky to have him as a dad, and so forth. I happen to find an attentive, involved, and loving spouse very attractive, but I need to say it out loud so that my spouse knows how attractive it is and to please keep it up!

My relationship with my husband is so much more complicated than I ever thought it would be, but I am also becoming so much more open to his needs because of the challenges we have had. To learn what my partner truly desires, and not to be able to fix it with gifts, exotic vacations, or even time apart to reignite our passion has made us dig very deep in our emotional well. And we have come up with buckets full of surprises amid all of the challenges and doubts. We get to be parents together, which is one of the reasons we chose to get married, and we get to love each other in a whole other way now, with the combinations of our genetic codes and all of our hard work and love cracking us up as they run around the house at full speed—naked—while growling like wild boars. Isn't that what a relationship should look like? We are pretty sure the answer is yes.

Things to Remember

This won't last forever. I know it sounds cliché, but I am going to say it anyway. I bet it feels eternal right now, right? Especially the first days, weeks, months, and year. Being a new parent feels like time has stopped and every minute takes forever. Changing a diaper on a squirmy newborn doesn't actually take ninety minutes; it takes more like five. But those five can really stretch out in your mind. Time does some weird bending and twisting and elongating when you are a new parent, and when I am unhappy, every setback, every disappointment, and every challenge feels like it lasts a lot longer and feels more oppressive than it really is.

I have to remind myself—sometimes numerous times in a day or an hour—that this may feel like it is going to last forever, but it won't. When I hear friends planning a fun-filled weekend in Las Vegas, I still get a twinge of longing. When I see an ad for a movie that I really want to see on the big screen right when it comes out, I sigh deeply. And I cannot count the number of wedding speeches I have missed hearing, not to mention the number of wedding cakes I have not eaten a slice of, because by the time said cake was served, I was already home and in my pj's, tucking the boys into bed and dozing off myself.

This is a phase of life. It won't last forever, and you will soon be looking for the moments that you get to share now with your children. It will all pass and it will all be okay.

Strong relationships will weather any storm. I was one of the first of my close circle of friends to have kids. My oldest son was born in October, and that first holiday season was a shock. I turned down so many invitations to holiday parties and events. I felt isolated, left out, and like an imprisoned woman. Friends who did not yet have kids seemed astonished that I would miss out on all of this fun simply because I had a baby who "needed" me so much (*Too much?* I wondered). Those same friends have kids now, and when I see them with their newborns they have the same haggard look I did. They get it now.

Sometimes months will go by without my seeing a friend who lives ten minutes away, with whom I used to go out weekly. It is incredible but true. I get to take care of my life and my kids as I best see fit. And my friends get to do the same for their lives and their families. Good friends who are reasonable and mature will be okay with the changes to your relationship. Others may not be able to stay as connected, but that's also okay. Relationships change over time anyway, and sometimes having kids forces changes. Strong relationships will endure these challenges, and you will grow from them. I have much richer connections with certain friends now that we are parents together, even if we do things differently. And the relationship with my husband is also stronger through the changes, with a lot of patience, negotiation, and compassion.

The Big Picture

Remember that everything we do as parents should keep the big picture in mind. Immediate gratification is just that; it's immediate. Raising kids takes a long-term commitment to shift your life to fit theirs into yours. It's okay to feel left out of things. It won't harm you or your relationships irreparably. Get help from a professional if you are struggling in your marriage. Don't foster unhealthy relationships with people who make you feel guilty or wrong for making the choices you make. Find friends who support you and can model healthy relationships for you.

And know that raising securely attached children who look to you for love, support, and advice as children and when they become adults will prove your doubts wrong. You can "have it all" in this sense: connection, camaraderie, and contentment, and you don't have to sacrifice your family's health or your needs to get those. Be realistic, be gentle with yourself, and consider letting your gym membership lapse. Matter of fact, why don't you take that money and put it toward a big TV, comfy pj's, and some fuzzy slippers? Those will serve you well right now.

13

Balancing Work and Family:
Different Families, Different Choices

In 1958, when La Leche League International published the first edition of *The Womanly Art of Breastfeeding*—their groundbreaking treatise on the mechanics and benefits of a parenting style that centered around breastfeeding—their chapter on the subject of whether or not mothers should return to work could have been practically one word long: "Don't." Their reason was not simply that work and breast-feeding were difficult to manage (which indeed they can be!). Rather, in the 1950s, the notion of being a complete and present parent did not include being physically apart from your child.

Almost fifty-five years after *The Womanly Art of Breastfeeding* was published, the world is a very different place for women and their families. At the dawn of the twenty-first century, about 75 percent of mothers work outside of the home, compared with approximately 35 percent in the 1950s. The women's liberation movement of the 1970s has led to generations of women being raised to find tremendous value and fulfillment by working outside of the home. In addition, a 2005 census review cited 51 percent of mothers who are single, and 63 percent of women find themselves as either the primary or equal breadwinner in their households, a figure not even documented in 1958!

It is not the purpose of this book to debate the decisions individual women make about working once they have children, nor is it my intention to imply that anyone is less of a mother for choosing to do so. What I will speak from is the experience of my family, and the experience of families I know who have placed the principles of attachment parenting at the foundation of all other decisions that they make, including the decision of who will work, when, where, how, and even why.

The choice made revolving around how to finance a household, a lifestyle, and a growing family is a very personal one. I would like to explain a few of the components my husband and I have based our decisions on.

Development in the Formative Months

As this book has detailed, the first months of a baby's life are critical in many ways. The basis of a human's ability to bond well as an adult can be traced back to the development in the first months of their infancy, as is an ability to trust, to love, and to soothe and be soothed. In addition, the establishment of a strong nursing relationship depends largely on the frequency and duration of nursing, usually to the exclusion of bottles and pacifiers. Because of this, frequent access to mother's breast on demand is your best bet for a good milk supply and a baby who gains enough weight for optimal development. Much as I consider myself a liberated woman who believes that men and women both can care for infants, it appears that to a large degree (outstanding or medically unavoidable factors aside), the first choice for a caregiver in the first months—some might argue the first *years*—of a baby's life is a mother. In fact, even if a mother does not breastfeed, a mother is still nature's preferred choice in the formative months of a baby's life.

This is not to say that men cannot parent well, nor is it to imply that babies cannot thrive under the eye of a caregiver other than the mother. I am simply speaking from the perspective of how nature designed us. This scientific fact fueled my decision not to pursue a career in academia beyond my doctorate. I knew that a job that required me to return to work after six weeks of maternity leave could in no way accommodate the kind of parenting I wanted to do. My husband agreed, and even on his best days with our sons while one of them was still nursing, when he sometimes cared for them for eight to ten hours while I was filming, he would sporadically report that at least once a day there would come a point when someone would want Mama for either nursing, holding, or soothing, and Dada just would not do. He found this a humbling experience even as he found it terribly frustrating. As he explained it, even if he had bottles of my milk, snacks galore, a fun and distracting many-hour outing to a museum or park or play date with a good solid uninterrupted nap in the car on the way home, there came a point when a baby wanted Mama, cried for Mama, and was not easily soothed until Mama would walk through the door. How much more this is true in the first months when baby does not yet have the words to express it! Like it or not, "biology is destiny" be cursed; sometimes only Mama will do.

You Can't Be in Two Places at Once

This sounds so simple that I almost feel silly mentioning it. But it bears repeating: much as you want to believe you can have it all and work at a great job and come home and be everything for everyone and make it all work and have a healthy dinner cooked every night and work out in your living room when the kids are sleeping and then have great sex with your energetic and receptive spouse before sleeping eight hours blah blah blah . . . it's just not going to happen that way.

The myth of being able to have it all is just that: a myth. I like to say that *doing* it all better describes my life rather than *having* it all does. You cannot work full-time and have the household of someone who doesn't. You cannot spend time and money on out-of-the-house activities by yourself in order to relax and wonder why everyone is so stressed out when you get home. And you cannot have the life of a childless dual-income family when you have children; it's just not possible.

I worry when people make plans to be twelve places in one day and then find it hard to understand why they are frazzled at home, impatient with their kids, and intolerant of their spouses' quirks or angry about how they incorrectly load the dishwasher. The decision you make about what work looks like in your family is a very complicated one, and I warn you against assuming that life can continue as it did before, just plus small people; it's not that simple.

Giving up the hope that you can have it all will probably give you a more realistic starting place to make decisions from. Remember that whatever you decide or plan, leave out the part where every day you feel thrilled and blessed that you have succeeded in having it all. Sorry to break it to you, but that day might not come for a few years!

Lifestyle Choices

People tell me a lot how lucky I am to parent the way I do. When I first heard this, I was very flattered. I assumed people meant that I was lucky to have been able to research my pregnancy, labor, and early childhood parenting style choices, to execute them with the support of doctors and midwives we trust, and to have a husband who is on board and willing to stay home with our boys. And I *do* consider myself lucky for all of those reasons.

What I have come to understand that most people mean, though, when they tell me how lucky I am is that they believe that I am lucky to effortlessly live this way, to have a husband who doesn't "need" to work to make money (or who just does whatever I tell him to, which is *so* far from the truth!), and that my acting career earns me so much money that I can afford the luxury of this green-chic lifestyle that I get to write books about.

Well, I hate to burst your bubble, but we don't parent this way because we can afford to; we parent this way because, like the thousands and thousands of families who share an attachment-theory-centered holistic philosophy, *we believe in it*. That means that we make choices about who works when and where based on our parenting decisions, not on our income. Families who believe in home birth, extended breastfeeding, and even homeschooling are, by and large, not wealthy. They are making the decision to parent this way out of conviction and not out of financial comfort!

I do not purport that our way of life is the best way. I know many dual-income couples who are wonderful parents and loving, intelligent people. However, I take issue with dual-income couples who tell me I am "lucky" to parent this way when I see that they enjoy a lot of the niceties that my husband and I go without—by choice. For example, we don't have fancy cars. (We have debated getting by with one car, in fact.) We don't pay for a nanny or a babysitter, and we don't go out to expensive meals. We don't go on vacations unless they are attached to speaking engagements that fund those trips as family adventures. We don't buy expensive foods; we buy simple foods that we try to make go a long way because we have a budget and we keep to it.

When you become a parent, get honest. What do you *want* and what do you *need*? What are you willing to give up? What can you live without? How can life go on as enjoyable and fulfilling without all of the stuff you are accustomed to? It can. Every family makes decisions about what their life will look like, and we all need to own those decisions. Should you decide that you want to use your money to take luxury vacations, buy fancy sports cars, and eat out at the hippest places in town with frequency, that's fine. But be honest about your choices, and just as you don't want to be judged by those of us who choose to go without, don't assume we are self-righteous martyrs. Everyone does this life differently, and I try to allow everyone the dignity to make their choices without my tsk-tsking them. Usually, I succeed!

How I've Done It

I know you are wondering about "us." Me and my husband and how we work this parenting thing out. You may wonder what my husband is like, how he handles my working, and how a marriage survives a woman as the primary breadwinner.

Well, my husband is a very humble, proud, stoic man. He is not particularly warm and fuzzy. He doesn't like talking about himself, nor does he open up easily about his feelings. He is masculine but not brutish and sensitive but not passive. Fortunately, he had a wonderful role model for a dad in his father. When my husband and his brother were little, my father-in-law was loving, creative, present, and committed to his sons, and I am grateful to have such a father-in-law. In addition, my husband's mother was and is a very self-sufficient woman who can just as easily fix a radiator as she can whip up stuffed acorn squash and an adorable little Jell-O mold with a parsley sprig on top. From my mother-in-law, my husband learned to be self-sufficient, hard-working, and very devoted.

All that being said, it is indeed a challenge when the traditional roles society sees as "normal" are reversed—even when both parties are on board. My husband gets asked a lot of very personal questions all the time about his desires, his needs, and his feelings regarding being the at-home dad. He finds it somewhat offensive that moms aren't asked the things he is: he is asked if he feels he is missing out on life, if he has lost his dreams, and if he wishes he could hire someone to take care of the kids for him. He feels that our children are his job now, and given our circumstances, they are as much his responsibility and blessing as they are mine. I am proud to have married such a man.

Do we have struggles about it? Yes. Is it hard sometimes? Yes. Do I feel pressure to earn enough to keep us satisfied? Of course. But we believe that our choices for now are our best chance for the outcome we desire. It's sort of just that simple. All of the what-ifs disappear when you constantly remind yourself that your kids are what it's about. Not the fancy car, the new bathroom flooring you covet (okay, that's me doing the coveting, not him), the all-expenses-paid trip for two to the Virgin Islands that we have not been able to cash in for two years running. It is about what is best for our children and our family. Case closed.

When our boys were tiny, I was rarely away from them, and I mean this very literally. When I was in graduate school and had Miles, I was done with coursework, so he joined me on trips to my lab and was with me as I worked from home, often nursing as I ran data analyses and edited my thesis on my laptop. Miles was still nursing well into the time I was completing my thesis work, and by the end of my seven years as a graduate student, I needed larger blocks of time in which to finish editing my thesis uninterrupted. The problem was that Miles never took a bottle, so my husband would plan around his nursing schedule, running out of the house with him right after a nursing and returning home when he needed to nurse again. Much as my husband appreciated and valued our nursing lifestyle, this period of time was somewhat of a challenge for him, since he and Miles could not be away from me for very long! It was at this time that he and Miles began a new phase of their relationship, and they began having outings that let me work on my thesis for stretches of first four, then five, and eventually six hours. It was in this way that I completed my thesis, just in time to get pregnant with Fred.

Once Fred was out of the newborn phase and nursing was well established, I started going on auditions. We four did it together: we all went in the car to my auditions, Fred screaming the entire way since he hated the car seat with the passion only a newborn can express. I would run in to my audition, be gone anywhere from ten to twenty minutes, and then I would nurse Fred again and we would all drive home together, Fred screaming all the way home. That routine was how I scored my first acting work since I was a teenager, and by the time I got the audition for my role on *The Big Bang Theory*, Fred was old enough to hang out with his big brother and his dad at home. (Perhaps his *not* screaming in the car was better pre-audition relaxation than I had experienced in the past. . . .)

Throughout Fred's second year, I was working semiregularly on *The Big Bang Theory* and still nursing. I pumped every two to three hours that I was away from Fred, and my husband gave him bottles of my milk while handling the daily routine of taking the boys to the park, on errands, to the market, and to Miles's homeschool activities. When I am not working, we either do these things together, or my husband gets time away from the kids to do errands, do things for himself, or sleep in! In general, we do most of the caregiving side by side, and it is a really neat way to parent, even though it's also very unusual and there are often more opinions than one needs about mundane issues such as: should we wash the sheets on warm or hot, should we have avocado or almond-butter sandwiches for lunch, and does Fred's potty need to be emptied every single time he pees or is every other time sufficient? Sometimes we need to remind ourselves to have a sense of humor; too many cooks can indeed spoil the pot(ty).

I like to do most of the cooking in our family whether I am working or not, but my husband has really stepped up to the plate since I have been working more, and he even joined me and the boys in our vegan food choices, which has been a new way for him to think and cook. We recently (it took seven years of marriage to figure this out!) divided up chores so that my husband does the two most incessant chores, dishes and laundry, while I handle the bigger but less frequent jobs such as bathrooms, sweeping, mopping, and toy cleanup/organization (which I actually love). This distribution of chores has helped reduce our stress and struggles a lot.

When I work, I am typically away three half days a week, and two days of the week I work ten- to twelve-hour days, which are hard for us all. It's a long time for my husband to be on full duty, and it's a long time for me to be away, since I miss the boys and, when I was pumping, that was not as much fun as nursing, for me or Fred! In addition, I usually have been the one responsible for nighttime duties, including nursing our little guy to bed, so my long work days present a challenge for my husband, who most nights is in charge of reading to our older son and helping him drift off to sleep without also tending to a baby who typically needs to nurse to fall asleep. When my husband is on double duty, he stands and paces as he rocks Fred while singing out loud for both boys' benefit, and hopefully he can lull both to sleep at roughly the same time. Once our little guy is asleep, however, he typically cannot be put down without waking up, so I often come home to a sweaty husband because of the sleepy little man glued to his chest.

We are often asked how my husband relaxes or winds down after these kinds of days. Truth be told, the way he winds down is to be away from the house and away from anyone asking him for anything, and I don't blame him. He tells me that he likes to be among "adults in the real world," so he reads at coffee shops and sometimes sees friends. He also enjoys watching sports and a variety of TV shows, and this is something I have noticed is often more important for him than hearing about my day, at least immediately. There are men who like to talk and listen and process their own feelings as well as those of their wives, and then there are men who like to watch sports and not have to chitchat a lot. I got the latter and I am okay with that. I am grateful for him and very appreciative of him. A present father is very attractive and desirable!

Some Other Families Who Are Making It Work

Our situation is unusual. I know that. And although I can't be certain, there are probably only a handful of people reading this book whose lives look like ours in terms of division of labor, scheduling around network executives, and planning around sitcom tapings. I am fully aware that our specific situation, while interesting, may not be helpful to most people when discussing how to make attachment parenting work while still working.

What I have decided to do is highlight the lifestyles of several of my closest friends—anonymously, of course—who utilize the parenting I describe in this book while still making ends meet. None of the friends I will describe are independently wealthy or get financial support from anyone but themselves, none have nannies, none have anyone but their spouses and children living in their homes, none utilize the services of a regular babysitter nor have they ever used day care, and none have family in the city where they live. (You can see why I am friends with them—they are just like me!) One or two may splurge on help with cleaning the house, and all have suggested that I do the same, but that's not the point. Two of the families I will discuss have two homeschooled school-age children, and the other family has a not yet school-aged child, so no one I discuss is getting manicures or taking long naps while the kids are at school—their kids are never at school! And for the record, none of these families would be considered wealthy by American standards.

I present the lives of three families here, but I actually know many more that would fit into each of these categories. There are numerous ways to have this style of parenting work—not just these three options—and the choices you make depend on a lot of factors, including what part of the country you live in and what the cost of living is there. I have chosen to refer to these lifestyles according to the cocktail order that their lives most resemble. My husband told me that I can't call anyone "on the rocks" even as a joke, so I present to you: straight up with a twist, blended, and shaken, not stirred.

Straight up with a twist

This family has a full-time stay-at-home mom who is the primary caregiver. She does the majority of the cooking and cleaning, as well as the shuttling around of the kids to their various activities. Dad works most weekdays and sometimes has to work on weekends. When Dad is home, he sometimes shares in responsibilities such as bathing the kids and helping put the older son to bed. Although he is not the primary caregiver and is much less involved in the details of the children's lives than the mother, Dad has enough knowledge of the family structure to stay at home with the boys for an evening, and Mom has even been away for a few several-day trips a year once her boys were no longer nursing at night.

That's the "straight up" part. The "twist" is that this particular mom has artistic talents with which she does freelance work. This work is sometimes done with her kids in tow, but most often she works either when her husband can get a half day off from work, or on a weekend when he is not working. Because her boys have such active schedules, it is generally difficult for her to leave them in the care of a friend, but it can be done, and we have had success taking turns watching each other's kids. We both need the help, so this has worked out great.

The atmosphere in the "straight up with a twist" family is that everyone is always working very hard: Mom is working hard with the boys, Dad is working a steady job and then he is also with the boys so Mom can get a break. As it turns out, the time Mom *does* get off is often spent working on her freelance career. However, she feels empowered and fulfilled when she gets to do her own thing, especially since it is a creative outlet. She is valued as an artist, teaches her craft in our homeschool community, and still has the benefit of raising her kids without day care or formal schooling, which is her passion and preference. Because this couple has more of a traditionally accepted "pattern" in their marriage, there is not the tension I described that my husband and I feel. However, there is not a tremendous amount of room for date nights, nor has this couple been away without their kids since before they had them! The children in this family are thriving and creative, intelligent and scholastic. It works for them.

Blended

When I say this next family is blended, I don't mean that they have children from previous marriages. I mean that they blend the work duties in a way that meets the needs of their son and family very well, while still providing more than one income. Once Mom got pregnant, she worked very hard with her boss to arrange a schedule that would allow her to work from home after the baby arrived, and this arrangement has even continued as she has moved all over the country with her husband and son.

Mom is at home with the little one all day, but for about four hours of each day she has a skilled mother's helper to care for her son in the home. A mother's helper is the old-fashioned term for a young woman who does not take the place of the mother by acting as primary caregiver, but rather helps the mother get things done so that she can still be the primary caregiver for her child; doing dishes, laundry, and basic cleanup are often included in job responsibilities. Mother's helpers traditionally were younger women or teenagers, but now the term can apply to any person helping a mom who still is the primary caregiver.

For the particular mom I am describing, her work involves a lot of time on the computer and phone and she can be interrupted if the need arises. This mother's helper brings the baby to Mom for nursings or comfort if the child cannot be comforted otherwise, and Mom can even take part in feedings and naps while still being able to do her work. Dad works six days a week but is on baby duty when he gets home so that Mom can get in a few more hours of work after the mother's helper has gone home. Mom is primarily responsible for cooking and cleaning, but even a few hours for a break at the end of her day helps her unwind, recharge, or get more done, depending on what is called for!

As with our first family, Mom rarely is getting time "for her," since her time away from the baby is primarily spent working to earn money for the family. You can probably guess that this couple does not spend a lot of time on dates or at luxury resorts. They have been able to go on a few dates when Grandma has visited, but for the most part, their commitment is to a lifestyle of raising a securely attached child. Indeed, he is thriving, healthy, active, and curious. It's working for them.

Shaken, not stirred

Picture a bartender at a bar on a tropical island, putting various liquids into a silver canister, placing a glass over the canister, turning it upside down, and shaking it vigorously. That's a little bit what our last couple's life is like. In this remarkable scenario, Mom was home for the first several months of both of her children's first years, at which point she returned to work from about 6 a.m. to 3 p.m. every day, not without a lot of mixed emotions. During the time Mom is at work, Dad takes care of the kids and does most of the cooking and cleaning as well. Like my husband, this dad takes the kids to their activities, runs errands, and gets the house ready for Mom to come home to. Once she is at home and on the weekends, Dad is pretty much off duty and Mom takes over, acting as the 100 percent at-home mom. Whereas my husband and I tend to mix it all up by sharing responsibilities simultaneously, this couple really does more of what you might call tag-team parenting. Sometimes I see them together, but the way that Dad unwinds is to do a lot of stuff separate from the family. He is an artist and has a lot of outside interests. He is very handy and crafty and often spends "his" time making and fixing things. In addition, this couple owns and rents out a duplex that the dad is responsible for managing.

This mom and dad carve out time for themselves when they can, but rarely do they get time alone. They went on their first night away in four years by leaving their children with a trusted relative who lived near the hotel they chose to stay at. They were the first of our little group of friends to do a romantic getaway, as it were, and when they returned, we ladies giggled and questioned their activities as if we had just encountered the first people who had been to Mars.

This couple has a lot of the same struggles that my husband and I do, largely because society is surprised when a man is the primary at-home parent. Additionally, men like my husband and this dad, who were not raised with the mind-set of being an at-home dad, need time to adjust to the expectations, and I think that even the most committed man has a reckoning of sorts associated with this. Truth be told, in this couple, Mom wishes she could be home, but since she is the more significant earner for now, this situation is in the best interest of their family. Their children are cared for differently by the dad than they would be by the mom, but they are amazing, inquisitive, unique, and loving children who are doing great. It's working for them.

We Can Work It Out

I hope that this discussion of ways to practice attachment parenting while balancing work has not overwhelmed you. The realization that the first months and years of a child's life are incredibly significant should not come as a surprise to you, but the emphasis that many of us who parent this way place on this fact may be daunting. As parents, we have so much power, such ability to shape a life, and such tremendous responsibility to make this person the best person that he or she can be.

Now is the time to take a look at your life and see where you can stop saying "I can't" and start saying "I can." And now is also the time to be honest about what you want life to look like. Some new parents have a distinct moment of clarity and decide to shift their priorities, finding ways to make it happen with courage, creativity, and patience. These people reach out to others who they see are living a life that they desire, and they seek out help to make their lives closer to their ideal. I never would have imagined that a life so drastically different from the one that I loved before I became a mother could be so beautiful, so lovely, and so satisfying, even despite the things I miss. I am grateful to the families who are walking this path with us. They give me confidence, loving support, and healthy role models. It's also a great reality check when I am feeling low, because I know I am not alone and it will be okay.

There are also those parents who do not want to give up the lifestyle that they enjoyed before they had children. They use their financial resources to facilitate the things that they enjoyed before they had kids, and they either are happy or they aren't. When I hear of people living this way who feel guilty and like they are messing up an opportunity to be present, I try to gently point out that at any time you can take a step back and reassess what you are doing. There are changes you can make that can help you feel good about being present. You would be amazed at the things you can go without, and you can also feel a whole new universe of great about being the parent nature intended you to be.

You cannot be in two places at once. You cannot make milk from a formula that's exactly the same as milk from your breast. You cannot make *watching a video* of your child taking his first steps exactly the same thing as *seeing* your child take his first steps.

Something's gotta give. But I guarantee you that when something gives—be it the trips to Mexico, the expensive champagne, the massages at the spa—you will get so much more than you have given up. Give up, give in, and give yourself a chance to work hard to find what works.

Resources

Chapter 1: You Know More Than You Think

Books:

Sears, William, MD, and Martha Sears, RN. *The Baby Book: Everything You Need to Know About Your Baby from Birth to Age Two.* New York: Little Brown and Company, 2005. This book was the always-out, always-handy "bible" for the first year of our sons' lives. It contains everything from the basics of birth and nursing to nutrition and growth charts, discipline suggestions, and troubleshooting for sleep, digestive, and behavioral problems. Dr. Sears is a known advocate of attachment parenting but is very open to all styles of parenting. Martha Sears is an international, board-certified lactation consultant (IBCLC) and nurse. This book will help you no matter the parenting style you choose!

Feder, Lauren, MD. *Natural Baby and Childcare: Practical Medical Advice and Holistic Wisdom for Raising Healthy Children.* Long Island City, NY: Hatherleigh, 2006. This is an additional excellent reference that describes a holistic approach to parenting, with an emphasis on both presenting conventional and alternative methods of medical care.

Chapter 2: What Is Attachment Parenting? The Science of Attachment and Intuition

Books:

Sears, William, MD, and Martha Sears, RN. *The Attachment Parenting Book: A Commonsense Guide to Understanding and Nurturing Your Baby.* New York: Little Brown and Company, 2001. This is a concise and elegant explanation of the main tenets and benefits of attachment parenting.

Nicholson, Barbara, and Lysa Parker. *Attached at the Heart: 8 Proven Parenting Principles for Raising Connected and Compassionate Children.* iUniverse Star, 2009. Written by the co-founders of Attachment Parenting International, this lovely book provides extensive research and practical suggestions for how to make the commitment to attachment parenting every day.

Organizations:

Holistic Moms Network, www.holisticmoms.org: HMN is a nonprofit organization for parents interested in holistic health and green living. They encourage trusting your instincts and using an innate sense of what is best for your children, living in balance with the earth, and learning about the pros and cons of all health care and parenting options. Everyone is welcome at HMN, no matter where you are in your parenting journey.

Attachment Parenting International, www.attachmentparenting.org: API is a non-profit organization that promotes parenting practices that create strong, healthy emotional bonds between children and their parents. Through education, support, advocacy, and research, API emphasizes the profound significance of secure attachment with an interest in reducing and ultimately preventing emotional and physical mistreatment of children, addiction, crime, behavioral disorders, mental illness, and other outcomes of early unhealthy attachment.

Mothering magazine (Mothering.com), published in print from 1976 until 2010, recognizes parents as the experts on their children and is the authority on the natural family lifestyle. *Mothering* was the only independently owned family-living magazine in the world and is now available as an excellent online resource, as they address contemporary health, personal, environmental, medical, and lifestyle issues.

Chapter 3: Baby Needs a Smooth Entrance: Birth

Books:

England, Pam and Rob Horowitz. *Birthing from Within: An Extra-Ordinary Guide to Childbirth Preparation.* Partera Press, 1998. This is a guidebook that walks you through pregnancy with a holistic flair: it contains writing exercises, art projects, and techniques for understanding pain and labor that many women find tremendously helpful.

Gaskin, Ina May. *Ina May's Guide to Childbirth.* New York: Bantam, 2003. A modern perspective on what happens in birth and labor and how to prepare for the birth you want, whether in a hospital, birth center, or at home. This book is very accessible to women of all backgrounds and lifestyles, and it was the birth stories in this book that I read the night before my second son was born.

Birth Wish List (previously referred to as a birth plan):
Here is an excellent free online birth wish list. Fill it in and print up three copies. www.earthmamaangelbaby.com/free-birth-plan.

Doulas:
Doulas of North America: www.dona.org.

Midwives:
The American College of Nurse-Midwives: www.midwife.org.

Films:
Lake, Ricki, and Abby Epstein. *The Business of Being Born* (New Line Home Video, 2008). www.thebusinessofbeingborn.com.

Hypnosis:

Many women love the popular and respected Hypnobabies hypnosis program (www.hypnobabies.com); I used a similar but more self-directed program called Hypbirth (www.hypbirth.com/fr_home.cfm). No matter what program you decide to explore, the principle of each is the same. The variables are how much you want to pay and whether you are interested in group classes. Find the one that fits your lifestyle best!

Chapter 4: Baby Needs Milk: Why We Breastfeed

Films:

Breastcrawl.org is the site that has video of newborns crawling on their moms in order to latch on and nurse for the first time.

Books:

Bengson, Diane. *How Weaning Happens.* La Leche League International, 2000. This guide explains the principles, benefits, and practical aspects of child-led weaning. The book can be used by moms who want to keep nursing, moms who are interested in weaning slowly, or moms who are seeking to wean altogether.

Bumgarner, Norma J. *Mothering Your Nursing Toddler.* La Leche League International, 2000. This friendly book examines why babies like to nurse into toddlerhood, why it's important to continue nursing if you and your nursling are happy, and how to make nursing a toddler enjoyable, pleasant, and beneficial for all. For those of us who believe in letting toddlers nurse, the support you gain from reading other moms' stories is tremendously helpful.

Wiessinger, Diane, Diana West, and Teresa Pitman. *The Womanly Art of Breastfeeding,* 8th ed. New York: Bantam Books, 2010. First published by La Leche League International in 1958 but revised for twenty-first-century moms, this is the classic go-to standard for any and all breastfeeding questions, concerns, and support. This is a wonderful resource for any decisions you make about how to feed and nourish your child, and the eighth edition is especially sensitive and open to the lifestyles of modern families.

Moen, Cecilia. *Breastmilk Makes My Tummy Yummy.* Panama City, Florida: Midsummer Press, 1999. A hysterical cartoon-illustrated book of babies and toddlers nursing—our favorite children's book about nursing!

Olsen, Mary. *I'm Made of Mama's Milk.* Mary Olsen Books, 2002. A lovely book of photographs of a baby nursing and being held close by her parents as she grows.

Supplies:
Breast pads: I preferred nondisposable pads made of wool (LANA) or cotton, available on many green-parenting websites.

Nipple cream: Motherlove organic nipple cream was my favorite cream to use besides just using breastmilk; it is vegan and all-natural and does not need to be wiped off before nursing.

Clothing: There are numerous websites and catalogs from which you can order nursing clothing, but my favorite tanks were from Motherwear (motherwear.com).

Expressing breastmilk: The most widely referenced, simple, and efficient method of manually expressing breastmilk is the Marmet Technique, developed by Chele Marmet, IBCLC. Here is a link to an online tutorial: http://www.medelabreastfeedingus.com/tip-and-solutions/130/how-to -manually-express-breastmilk—the-marmet-technique.

Chapter 5: Baby Needs to Be Held: How Will You Ever Get Anything Done Ever Again?

Organizations that Support Babywearing:
La Leche League International: www.llli.org

Holistic Moms Network: www.holisticmoms.org

Attachment Parenting International: www.attachmentparenting.org

Slings I love:
Maya Wrap: Our go-to sling for newborn to toddler: www.mayawrap.com.

Ergo Carrier: A structured pack for hiking and longer adventures: *www .ergobabybcarrier.com.*

Moby Wrap: Some learning as to how you want to tie it is necessary, but it is very strong, comfortable, and easy: www.mobywrap.com.

Other sources:
Babywearing International (http://babywearinginternational.org) promotes babywearing as a universally accepted practice through education and support. Their website has great resources for choosing the carrier that is right for you.

Mothering.com features a babywearing section of their online community (http://www.mothering.com/babywearing) with a variety of articles and information about why and how to wear your baby, including their 2010 award-winning article, which is available for reprint.

Chapter 6: Baby Needs Nighttime Parenting: Gentle Techniques and Co-sleeping

Books:
Goodavage, Maria, and Jay Gordon, MD. *Good Nights: The Happy Parents' Guide to the Family Bed (and a Peaceful Night's Sleep!).* New York: St. Martin's Griffin, 2002. This is one of the simplest and best explanations of the whys and hows of the family bed I have read. It is fact-based, fun, and practical without being preachy or judgmental.

McKenna, James, MD. *Sleeping with Your Baby: A Parents' Guide to Cosleeping.* Platypus Media, 2007. McKenna is one of the most vocal and respected voices in the co-sleeping and attachment parenting community. He is a world-renowned anthropologist specializing in primate social behavior, sleep, and breastfeeding, and he is the director of the

Mother-Baby Behavioral Sleep Laboratory at the University of Notre Dame.

Articles:

Katherine A. Dettwyler, PhD, "Sleeping through the Night," http://www.kathydettwyler.org/detsleepthrough.html. This is an incredible article on co-sleeping by respected anthropology professor Katherine A. Dettwyler, who holds positions at both the University of Delaware and Texas A&M University. Her fields of study are cross-cultural and evolutionary perspectives on breastfeeding, weaning, and solids. Her website is also a great resource: http://www.kathydettwyler.org/dettwyler.html.

Products:

Arm's Reach Co-sleepers (*www.armsreach.com*) are one of the most popular bed attachments that facilitate co-sleeping, but there are many brands on the market that can meet your needs, depending on your desires for your sleeping environment, bed height, etc.

Safety guardrails and bumpers can be an inexpensive option for safe co-sleeping in a standard bed. These attach to the frame of any bed and are a great choice for older kids as well.

If you choose to bed-share, I cannot recommend the following website and product highly enough: www.humanityorganics.com. It features an organic cotton bed-top "family sleeper" that prevents roll-offs, absorbs breastmilk (or baby leaks), and contains a removable body pillow that is a great aid to comfortable sleeping when pregnant. This product was the answer to all of our bed-sharing woes!

Chapter 7: Baby Needs Potty: Elimination Communication

Books:

Bauer, Ingrid. *Diaper Free: The Gentle Wisdom of Natural Infant Hygiene,* 2nd ed. New York: Penguin, 2006. This is the simplest, least flashy, and most incredible book I have seen on EC. Ingrid Bauer effortlessly makes a beautiful case for why to practice EC and smoothly helps you make it happen no matter your preconceived notions, limitations, or fears. It is truly an eye-opening book that taught me much more than just how to practice EC; this book literally changed the way I viewed everything about being a parent.

Organizations:

Diaperfreebaby.org is a network of support groups and education about EC. It is a wonderful resource for people who EC part-time, full-time, or are just plain curious about EC.

Products:

You can purchase EC-friendly clothing, accessories, and potties from a variety of websites and stores, but here are the three main things we most frequently needed, all of which we got at TheECStore.com:

1. Inexpensive cotton prefold diapers. We purchased a dozen of these and used them tucked into a giant fleece scrunchie around the baby's waist, known colloquially as an EC belt.
2. Baby leg warmers. It was important that our babies be in EC-accessible attire while also staying warm. TheECStore.com often has great sales on less "trendy" colors and prints that do the trick just as well as the more trendy ones!
3. A tiny potty (or three). I found that having a potty in a few rooms made ECing much easier and more convenient.

Chapter 8: Baby Doesn't Need All That Stuff: Figuring Out the Essentials

There are no resources necessary for a chapter about eliminating "stuff"! However, the importance of a simple and elegant set of supplies for babies and children is described thoughtfully in this book: *You Are Your Child's First Teacher: What Parents Can Do with and for Their Children from Birth to Age Six,* Rahima Baldwin Dancy, Celestial Arts, 2000. The book includes suggestions for natural toys, creative and stimulating activities, and an approachable and intelligent analysis of the mental shifts required to change the way we view consumption and "stuff" in our society.

Chapter 9: Baby Doesn't Need Unnecessary Medical Intervention: When (and When Not) to Call the Doctor

Books:

Feder, Lauren, MD. *The Parents' Concise Guide to Childhood Vaccinations: Practical Medical and Natural Ways to Protect Your Child.* Long Island City, New York: Hatherleigh Press, 2007. This small book is designed for parent who choose to vaccinate (offering natural ways to avoid possible side effects), parents who don't vaccinate (suggesting natural ways to prevent sickness and treat it), and parents who are unsure what to do (presenting a balanced and truly impartial discussion of the effectiveness, pros, and cons of every single vaccine and illness). I recommend this book to anyone curious about the facts of vaccines; it's also a great book to hand to inquiring and/or skeptical family members who want to know about your decisions about vaccinations.

Also by Feder, Lauren, MD. *Natural Baby and Childcare: Practical Medical Advice and Holistic Wisdom for Raising Healthy Children from Birth to Adolescence.* Long Island City, New York: Hatherleigh Press, 2006. This is an excellent reference that presents alternative and conventional methods of treating any and every ailment, sickness, and boo-boo known to modern parents.

Sears, Robert, MD. *The Vaccine Book: Making the Right Decision for Your Child.* New York, New York: Little Brown, 2011. From the Dr. and Martha Sears pediatric dynasty of physicians comes a balanced book about the ups, downs, and alternative schedules available for families who do choose to vaccinate. The Sears are respected by attachment parents and non-attachment parents alike, since they are very supportive of the former without excluding the latter.

Magazines:
Lillipoh is a holistically oriented publication that focuses on alternative and naturopathic health treatments and philosophies: www.lilipoh.com/index.aspx.

Recipe for baby and children's shampoo
(adapted slightly from Mothering *magazine)*
Put 1 cup of water in a spray bottle. Add 3/4 cup any liquid castile soap (such as Dr. Bronner's plain castile soap), 2 teaspoons of carrier oil (such as almond, jojoba, or olive), and 10 drops of any essential oil you want. I like 4 drops each of lavender and bergamot, and 2 drops of tea tree oil, but experiment with whatever smells good to you. Shake to mix. If the mixture is too soapy, simply add more water to the spray bottle. This is *concentrated*, so one or two sprays is plenty for short hair. For shoulder-length hair, I use 4 to 5 sprays. This *is not* a "no tears" recipe, so flush with water if the shampoo gets into tender eyes!

Chapter 10: Baby Doesn't Need Pressure: Letting Kids Be Kids

Books:
Dancy, Rahima Baldwin. *You Are Your Child's First Teacher: What Parents Can Do with and for Their Children from Birth to Age Six*. Celestial Arts, 2000. Even if you don't subscribe to the philosophy of Rudolf Steiner, which is the basis of Waldorf education, this book introduces you to the concepts of the rhythms of babies and children, with an emphasis on allowing creativity to flourish uninterrupted in the first years of a child's life.

Organizations:
Magda Gerber started RIE (Resources for Infant Educarers), and although I don't agree with her all of the time, the concepts of the importance of observation and allowing children not to be hovered over constantly are a foundation of the way we parent: www.rie.org.

Chapter 11: Baby Doesn't Need Punishment: Understanding Gentle Discipline

The two parenting classes I mention in this chapter emphasize gentle discipline but have no "agenda" on a parenting style. Both are taught nationally by accredited instructors.

1. STEP: Systematic Training for Effective Parenting:
   www.steppublishers.com
2. Quality Parenting: Ilene Val-Essen, PhD: www.qualityparenting.com

Books:
Flower, Hilary. *Adventures in Gentle Discipline: A Parent-to-Parent Guide.* La Leche League International, 2005. This friendly guide to parenting with gentle discipline is full of anecdotes and user-friendly explanations of the philosophy, and paints a practical picture of the benefits, challenges, creativity, and resources needed in order to commit to parenting this way. The book is especially helpful because the parents who share their experiences are authentic and honest about what works for them and where they sometimes falter.

Bring Out the Best in Your Child and Yourself: Creating a Family Based on Mutual Respect, by Ilene Val-Essen, 2010, and the workbook used in the Quality Parenting workshops, *Bring Out The Best In Your Child And Yourself: The Wisdom and Skills You Need to Create the Family You Want,* Ilene Val-Essen, 1999. The basis of the philosophy this author describes is that of building a relationship of respect, trust, and love in a family that will endure throughout their lives. An examination of your own notions of how children should behave, an analysis about what works and what doesn't, and practical suggestions for creating the family you want and deserve make these books truly special and, in my opinion, indispensable.

Acknowledgments

This book is hardly original, save for the errors. I live and breathe in gratitude to the generations that came before me. They survived unimaginable challenges so that I could have the opportunities they never even thought to dream of. I know they are with me and I pray that I serve their memories well.

Thank you to my parents, Barry Eugene and Beverly Barbara, who are equal parts maddening and unbelievably amazing. A special thank-you to all of my extended family, especially the women in my family and my cousins Rebekah Goldstein and Chaviva Deri. Thank you to my in-laws, who have oftentimes been baffled and bewildered by me and my parenting style but have a tremendous capacity for grinning and bearing it—in particular, my microbiologist mother-in-law, Sherrie Nielsen Stone, who also provided editorial assistance.

Todah rabah to my unofficial editor, closest friend, and trusted confidante who inspires me with her courage, open-mindedness, and love, Elie's *Ima*, Adi Rubin. You are a true woman of valor.

Thank you to the people who have helped me to live this life in manageable ways with grace and dignity: Dr. Nancy, Kyrie Collins, Marti Kartalian, and my mentor, Shawn Crane.

Thank you to my mom's group, who lived the sentiments and struggles of this book along with me: Kristinha Anding, Lorrie Feinberg, Nancy Stringer, Natalie Wolff, and Denise Herrick Borchert, who also provided the photography for the interior and the cover. Thank you to the fathers I learn from: my courageous husband, Michael, as well as Larry, Tony, Walter, and the irreplaceable Jacob Gisis.

Thank you to the mothers who may not always agree with me but nonetheless have allowed me to test out my theories and techniques on them and their children: Dr. Lisa Aziz-Zadeh, Gale Brennan, Kari "Pitzy" Druyen, Caron Eule, Briana Landau, Nina Mercer, Mariana Roytman-Schiffner, Bahareh Rinsler, and Neha Shah. And thank you to our "wacky" Northern California friends who started us on this path of parenting intuitively, Allison and Hawk Chait, and Jazmin Hicks and David Basile: Look what you started!

Thank you to David "Uncle Vidi" Guerrieri, Dana Kowalski, and Katie Morrow, who don't yet have children but show our boys the love and care of family.

Thank you to the women of La Leche League International and the larger lactation-support world, who cheerfully examined my breasts any time I asked them to and never once laughed: Shawn Crane, Holly Hollander, Genevieve Colvin, Allison Gann, Anne Leyden, Kim McGarry, Yana Katzap-Nackman, and Gina Edwards, who also provided editorial assistance.

Thank you, Nancy Masotto and all of Holistic Moms Network, for assisting me in finding my tribe, supporting me as a mother, and allowing me to speak on behalf of "alternative" parents everywhere.

Thank you, Dr. Jay Gordon, our pediatrician, lactation consultant, and writer of the introduction to this book, rolled into one. Thank you to his nursing staff, especially lactation consultant Jennifer Davidson.

Thank you to Dr. Robert Sears and Martha Sears, for their thorough editing and fantastic support of this book. Thank you, Home Birth Service of Los Angeles: midwives Leslie Stewart and Catherine Williams, and our fantastic midwife's assistant, Cheryl Schroeder, who unwrapped Fred's umbilical cord and told me to reach down and catch my baby. Thank you to my first doula, Katie Smith, and my second doula/accupuncturist/now-midwife, Elizabeth Bachner, who also provided editorial assistance.

Thank you to our early childhood Waldorf instructor and guide, Mrs. Elizabeth Shahbazi, who taught me to trust both my instincts and hers.

Thank you, Matthue Roth, Deborah Kolben, and everyone at My Jewish Learning and Kveller.com, for helping me hone my writing style and find my voice.

Thank you to my wise, enthusiastic, sincere, gentle, and kind literary manager Anthony Mattero at Renaissance, for believing in me and encouraging me every time my tiny ego hesitated that what I have to say is worth putting out there. Thank you, Alan Nevins, at Renaissance, and thank you to everyone at Touchstone, most notably Stacy Creamer and my amazing editor (and new mama!) Michelle Howry. You have entrusted me with a mighty task and I am honored to take it on.

Thank you to the multi-talented Maia Rosenfeld, for bringing me along with you on this journey in so many ways. Thank you, Evan Corday, Kari Stringham, Meghan Mathes, and Lindsay Whitaker at Evolution Entertainment, and thank you to Brandy Gold and Marion Campbell at Talentworks.

I am blessed to have found people in this crazy city and industry who always tell me the truth with no sugar coating—even if it stings. And it does. These mighty women are Elizabeth Much and Heather Weiss at Much & House Public Relations, and my fifteen-years-ago gym buddy, now manager and friend, Tiffany Kuzon at Evolution Entertainment, who has guided my career so gently and wisely through both of our pregnancies and beyond.

Thank you, celebrity mamas Ali Landry and Teresa Strasser, for telling me I should write a book even though I thought you were nuts at the time.

And finally, to my study partners and faithful and loyal friends Allison Josephs (JewintheCity), my cousin Abby Margulies, David Sacks, Eric Kaplan, and Immanuel Shalev: thank you for helping me remember Who it's really all about.

Index

About the Author

Mayim Hoya Bialik is best known for her lead role as Blossom Russo in the 1990s television sitcom *Blossom* and her role as Amy Farrah Fowler on *The Big Bang Theory*. She earned a BS and a PhD in Neuroscience from UCLA. Mayim and her husband live in Los Angeles with their two sons: Miles, born in 2005, and Frederick, born at home (unassisted until the final push) in 2008. She writes regularly for Kveller.com and is the spokesperson for the Holistic Moms Network. Visit her at mayimbialik.net.